Middle Primary Pupil's Book

Nicky Souter
Frances Simpson

Hodder Gibson
2A Christie Street, Paisley, PA1 1NB

Acknowledgements

The publishers would like to thank the following individuals, institutions and companies for permission to reproduce copyright photographs in this book. Every effort has been made to trace and acknowledge ownership of copyright. The publishers will be glad to make suitable arrangements with any copyright holders whom it has not been possible to contact:

Page 3, top left © Stapleton Collection/Corbis; top right © Bettmann/Corbis; page 5, top and middle © NASA/SPL; bottom © Chris Madeley/SPL; page 6, top © NASA; page 8, top left, right and bottom right © NASA/ SPL; bottom left © Mark Garlick/ SPL; page 9, top and bottom left © NASA/SPL; top right © Mark Garlick/SPL; bottom right © Lynette Cook/SPL; page 10, top © David Ball/Corbis; page 12, bottom left © Derek Croucher/Corbis; bottom right © Science Museum/Science & Society Picture Library; page 13, top left © David Parker/SPL; top right © Martin Bond/SPL; middle and bottom left © NASA/SPL; middle right © David Ducros/SPL; page 20 © Robert Llewellyn/Corbis; page 21, top right © Gusto Productions/SPL; page 22, top right © PLI/SPL; bottom left © Tommaso Guicciardini/SPL; page 23, top left © Rosenfeld Images Ltd/SPL; bottom left © Lawrence Lawry/SPL; bottom right © Andrew Lambert Photography/SPL; page 26, bottom left © Wayne Shakell/Life File; bottom middle © Bernard Annebicque/Corbis Sygma; bottom right © Forestier Yves/Corbis Sygma; page 29, top left © Eye of Science/SPL; top right © ICI; page 30, top © Mike Evans/Life File; bottom left © Mimmo Jodice/Corbis; bottom right © George McCarthy/ Corbis; page 32, bottom left © Holt Studios Photograph Library; bottom right © Cynthia Diane Pringle/Corbis; page 33, top left © Alex Bartel/SPL; top right © Royalty-Free/Corbis; page 34, top © Bob Battersby/BDI Images Ltd; bottom © Pascal Goetgheluck/SPL; page 35, bottom © Layne Kennedy/Corbis; page 36, © BBC; bottom left © Bob Krist/Corbis; page 37, middle left © Andrew Lambert Photography; middle right © Picimpact/Corbis; page 38, bottom © NASA/SPL; page 39, © Rex Features; page 41, © Bruce Miller/Corbis; page 42, SOHO/ESA/NASA/SPL; page 54, © Hulton-Deutsch Collection/Corbis; page 56, © Bob Battersby/BDI Images Ltd; page 59, © Bob Battersby/BDI Images Ltd; page 61, top right © Gideon Mendel/Corbis; middle left © Royalty-free/Corbis; page 63, top right © Bob Battersby/BDI Images Ltd; page 64, © Gusto/SPL; page 65, top left © Annebicque Bernard/Corbis Sygma; top right © Jan Suttle/Life File; page 66, middle right © David Samuel Robbins/Corbis; page 67, bottom left © Pascal Goetgheluck/SPL; top left © Michael S. Yamashita/Corbis; page 73, photograph of Jaques Shove Halfpenny Board courtesy of 'wheesh.com'; page 75, top left © Bettmann/Corbis; top right © Glyn Kirk/Action Plus; page 76, top left and right © motoring picture library; page 77, top left © Randy Wells/Corbis; top middle © John Conrad/Corbis; middle left and right, bottom left and middle © Glyn Kirk/Action Plus; page79, top left © Bettmann/Corbis; top right © Sheila Terry/SPL; bottom left © Rex Features; page 86, © Still Pictures; page 87, left © Kenneth H. Thomas/SPL, right © Chris Mattison; Frank Lane Picture Agency/Corbis; page 88, top right © Lynda Richardson; middle left © Suzanne L. Collins (snake), David T. Roberts (gecko), Gusto (tortoise)/SPL; bottom left © VVG/SPL; bottom right © Aubrey J Slaughter (robin), Emma Lee (eagle), Wayne Shakell (duck)/Life File, John Conrad/Corbis (penguins); page 89, top right © George McCarthy/Corbis (squirrel), Kennan Ward/Corbis (polar bears), Gusto/SPL (human); middle left © Dr Morley Read (bat), Stephen Kraseman (deer), Alexis Rosenfeld (dolphin)/SPL, Emma Lee (dog), Cliff Threadgold (seal)/Life File, bottom right © Dale Boyer (kangaroo), William Ervin (ostrich/whale), Phil Dotson (salamander), Mark Smith (eel), Jeff Lepore (alligator)/SPL; page 92, top right © Andrew Ward (poppies), Nigel Shuttleworth (buttercups), Terry O'Brien (roses)/Life File; bottom right © Dr Jeremy Burgess/SPL; page 93, top left © Vaughan Fleming (lilies), Simon Fraser (Cactus)/SPL; middle right © J. H. Robinson/SPL; page 94, top left © Dr Jeremy Burgess/SPL; top right © Michael Leach/NHPA; bottom © Gregory Ochocki/SPL; page 95, © Claude Nuridsany & Marie Perennou/SPL (horsetails); © Alex Bartel/SPL (conifers); page 98, middle left © S. R. Maglione; bottom left © Adam Hart-Davis/SPL; middle right © Holt Studios Photograph Library; bottom right © PA Photos; page 99, top right © Tim Davis/SPL; bottom right © Natalie Kemf/Life File; page102, © Jan Suttle/Life File; page 106, © Holt Studios Photograph Library; page 108, top © TH Foto-Werbling/SPL; bottom © Still Pictures; page109, top © Ken Preston-Mafham/PREMAPHOTOS/Nature Photo Library; middle © Alexis Rosenfeld/SPL; bottom © Still Pictures; page 110, top © Tim Davis (wolf), Phil Dotson (elk)/SPL; bottom left © David Gifford/SPL; bottom right © Natural History Museum; page 111, © Glasgow Museums: Fossil Grove; page 112, top left © Martin Bond/SPL, John Wilkinson/Ecoscene/Corbis; top right © Roger Tidman/Corbis; bottom © AP Photos; page 113, top left © Dale C. Spartas/Corbis; bottom left © Chris Hellier/Corbis; right © Still Pictures; page 116, top right © John Heseltine/SPL; middle right © Kenneth H. Thomas/SPL; page 117, top left and top right © Andrew Ward/Life File; middle left © Mike Evans/Life File; bottom left © Gary Meszaros/SPL.

All other photos by the authors and Hodder Gibson.

Artworks by Tony Wilkins Design.

Cartoons by the Richard Duszczak Cartoon Studio Limited.

Orders: please contact Bookpoint Ltd, 130 Milton Park, Abingdon, Oxon OX14 4SB. Telephone: (44) 01235 827720. Fax: (44) 01235 400454. Lines are open from 9.00 - 6.00, Monday to Saturday, with a 24 hour message answering service. You can also order through our website www.hodderheadline.co.uk.

British Library Cataloguing in Publication Data
A catalogue record for this title is available from the British Library

ISBN 0 340 88316 2

Published by Hodder Gibson, 2a Christie Street, Paisley PA1 1NB. Tel: 0141 848 1609; Fax: 0141 889 6315; Email: hoddergibson@hodder.co.uk
First Published 2004
Impression number   10 9 8 7 6 5 4 3 2 1
Year   2009 2008 2007 2006 2005 2004

Cover photo from Lawrence Lawry/Science Photo Library
Typeset by Julie Martin Ltd
Printed in Italy for Hodder Gibson, 2a Christie Street, Paisley, PA1 1NB, Scotland, UK

Preface

To the pupil

Key to symbols

This book is full of symbols to help you learn and this is what they mean:

 – information to read

 – the meanings of words

 – topics to talk about

 – an activity to do

 – an important idea to learn

 – tips on how to study science safely

 – see what you have learned

To the teacher

The textbooks and teachers' guides for Science 5-14 have been written to match the science component of the revised Environmental Studies 5-14 National Guidelines. The Middle Primary Pupil's Book is intended to cover content mainly from level C, with some from levels B and D where it would provide coherence, continuity and progression.

The book is divided into three sections which correspond to the Knowledge and Understanding outcomes Earth and Space, Energy and Forces and Living Things and the Processes of Life.

As part of the 5-14 programme, pupils are encouraged to develop informed attitudes towards the environment around them. Chapters 19, 39 and 59 allow pupils to develop an understanding of the world in which they live and of current environmental issues.

Science provides a number of contexts for pupils to develop a wide range of skills. These skills are featured throughout the book and Investigating skills are specially featured in Chapters 20, 40 and 60.

This book provides opportunities for pupils to relate science to their everyday experiences and to their surroundings in Scotland. The group of 'science pupils' relates much of the content in a way that we hope children reading the book will find appealing. We hope that this book will stimulate interest and enjoyment in science from the middle primary stages that will endure throughout the pupils' lives.

Hodder's Science 5-14 series extends from Middle Primary to Secondary Two, has involved 6 authors in the preparation of pupil books, teachers' guides and assessment packs. The authors are grateful to the skilful editorial team at Hodder Gibson and to the countless numbers of pupils in primary school, teachers, student teachers, researchers and friends from outwith school education that have directly and indirectly influenced our thinking. We are indebted above all to our families who have patiently supported and encouraged us at each stage in the preparation of the series, and to our own childhood, where we started asking our own questions.

This book is for Scottish children to do the same.

Nicky Souter and Frances Simpson

Contents

Living Things and the Processes of Life

What is science?

Science and knowledge

Science gives us knowledge about forces, energy, earth, space and living things. We will give you some of that information.

We will provide a summary, the key points. We all make observations about the world. Geese fly north in the spring. Milk goes off if you leave it out of the 'fridge. The sun rises in the east and sets in the west. Science tries to explain these observations. Science depends on ideas. People's ideas are described in theories.

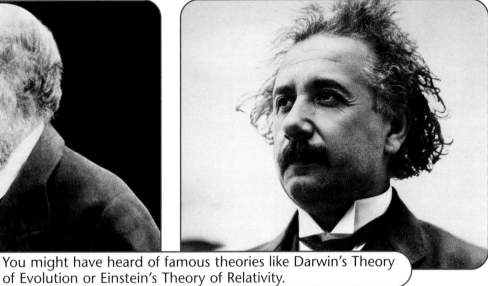

Figure 1 You might have heard of famous theories like Darwin's Theory of Evolution or Einstein's Theory of Relativity.

Thinking about science

Science is about asking questions.

We need to discuss our ideas and find out information from books and the Internet.

Doing science

Science is practical in order to test those ideas.

We will ask you to carry out activities and experiments. They must always be safe.

Where do we do science?

Science can be done at home, in school, outdoors or in special laboratories. It depends on what is being studied.

Key ideas

★ Science lets us find knowledge about things

★ Experiments and investigations help. So does finding out what other people know already

★ We can talk, listen, read and write about science

★ We can do science anywhere

2 Goodness gracious great balls of fire!

Four hundred years ago people believed that the **Earth** was the centre of everything. They thought the **Sun**, the **stars** and all the **planets** moved around the Earth in a great circle and that the Earth was the centre of the **Universe**. A famous scientist called **Galileo** thought they were all wrong and that the Sun was at the centre of our part of the Universe and that the Earth and planets all moved around the Sun. This seemed a terrible idea to most people and he was put into prison for saying such things.

The part of the Universe we live in is called the **Solar System**. At the centre of it is a star we call the Sun. There are nine planets travelling around the Sun. Our planet – we call it Earth – is the third planet out from the Sun.

Figure 1

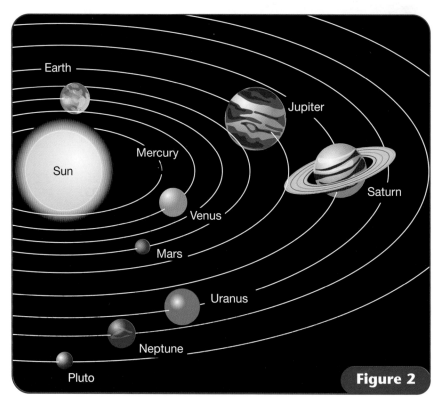

Earth

Jupiter

Sun

Mercury

Venus

Saturn

Mars

Uranus

Neptune

Pluto

Figure 2

Activity

Write down something you know about the Sun. Work in a group to put your ideas together. Now write some questions that you would like to ask about the Sun.

Have a look at the fact file on the opposite page – are the answers to your questions there?
If not, where could you find out?

Fact File

Name
The Sun

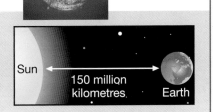

Type of object
Star

Distance from Earth
150 million kilometres

Sun ← 150 million kilometres → Earth

Size
One million four hundred thousand kilometres across

Size compared to Earth
100 times bigger

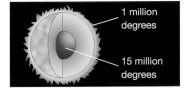

Earth   Sun

Temperature
Up to 15 million degrees Celsius in the middle

1 million degrees
15 million degrees

Made of
Burning gas causing atomic explosions

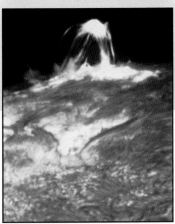

Features
Dark spots appear and solar flares – jets of flame can be seen shooting thousands of kilometres into space

Effect on Earth
Gives us light and heat. Solar wind causes auroras – glowing lights in the sky near the north and south poles of the Earth

Key ideas

★ The Sun is an ordinary and fairly small star in the Universe. It is a ball of very, very hot gas burning and exploding. It is huge and very far away.

Questions

1 Could you stand on the surface of the Sun? Why not?

2 Can you do a big sum? If the Sun was 150 million kilometres away and light travelled at a speed of 15 million kilometres every minute, how many minutes would it take light from the Sun to reach us on Earth?

5

3 Third rock from the Sun

We live on the third planet out from the Sun. We call our planet Earth.

Questions

1 People call this the 'Blue Planet'. What do you think makes it looks blue?

 Our planet is different from the others in the Solar system. It has a surface made of rock that is solid. Most of the surface of Earth is covered with a liquid called water, and above this is a layer of gas surrounding the whole planet. This is called the **atmosphere** and gives us the air we breathe.

Figure 1

The hard layer on the surface of the Earth is called the **crust**. Underneath this is a thick layer of very hot liquid rock. At the centre of the Earth is a solid ball of very hot iron.

Where did our planet come from? How was it made? How old is it?

Earth Facts	
Size	Distance to the centre of the Earth 6,400 km
Distance from the Sun	150 million km
Number of moons	1
Speed	Travels through space at about 30 km every second
Orbits the Sun	Once every 365 days

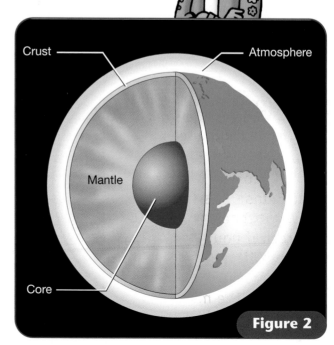

Crust — Atmosphere

Mantle

Core —

Figure 2

Spacecraft

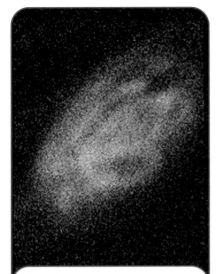

Figure 3A Earth started as a cloud of dust and gases.

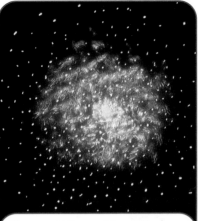

Figure 3B 4500 million years ago, the cloud slowly began to shrink and form a ball of hot, liquid rock and gas.

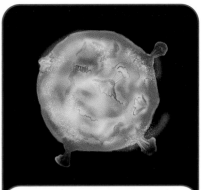

Figure 3C As the ball of rock cooled, the surface became solid although it was covered by erupting volcanoes. The whole planet was covered by a thick layer of cloud.

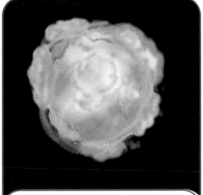

Figure 3D As the planet cooled, rain fell and formed the oceans. In some places the crust was thicker and stayed above the water making land.

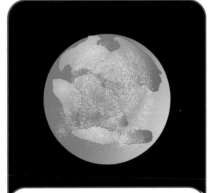

Figure 3E The areas of land have moved over the surface of the planet – 250 million years ago they formed one huge land we call Pangaea (pan-gee-ah).

Figure 3F The areas of land have drifted apart to make the world we know today.

Activity

Use some plasticine to make a model of Earth. Put a sphere together using lots of tiny balls of plasticine then roll it in your hands to smooth off the surface. Use some more flattened bits of plasticine to make continents, in green if you have it. Now use some thin pieces of blue plasticine to fill in the gaps between your continents. Take a long wooden kebab stick and slide it through the middle of your model so that you can spin it around like Earth.

Questions

1 If life began on Earth 3500 million years ago, how old was the Earth then?

2 Can you name three of the oceans and three of the continents on Earth?

4 Neighbours

Questions

1 There are nine planets travelling around the Sun. Can you name them all?

Our neighbour planets are all very different. Let me introduce you to them. We can see some of them as stars in the night sky but these pictures are taken through a telescope.

Figure 1 Mercury

Here's Mercury – the smallest planet and closest to the Sun. It looks a bit like our Moon. It's very hot and just a bare rocky surface.

Figure 2 Venus

Venus is the second planet out from the Sun. It has a hot dry surface beneath very thick clouds of a gas called carbon dioxide.

Figure 3 Mars

Earth is third from the Sun and beyond us is Mars. About half the size of Earth, Mars looks red because of the colour of its bare rocky surface. It only has a thin atmosphere of carbon dioxide gas.

Figure 4 Jupiter

This one's huge! Jupiter is the largest planet and is a bit like the Sun because it is mostly made of swirling gases. Jupiter has a huge red spot that moves about the surface. It is a swirling hurricane of gas moving at terrific speeds.

Literacy

The **atmosphere** is a layer of gas surrounding a planet.

Figure 5 Saturn

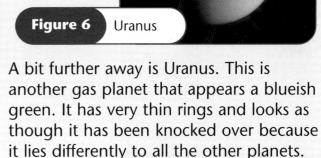

Figure 6 Uranus

Our prettiest neighbour, Saturn is like a smaller Jupiter but has rings surrounding it. These are made of bits of rock and ice. The centre of Saturn is a small solid core of rock.

A bit further away is Uranus. This is another gas planet that appears a blueish green. It has very thin rings and looks as though it has been knocked over because it lies differently to all the other planets.

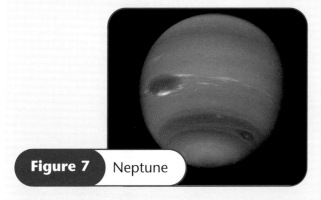

Figure 7 Neptune

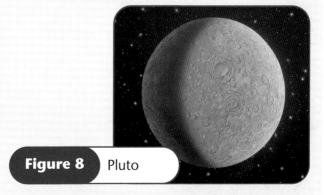

Figure 8 Pluto

Next comes Neptune. This is a gas planet too but appears more blue than Uranus and has no rings. Very strong winds carry clouds around it at great speeds.

Last comes Pluto – scientists think it might have been a moon of Neptune that was knocked out of orbit. It is probably solid with a frozen surface. It is so far from the Sun that it is very, very cold and dark.

Activity

Can you find out a few facts about each of the planets for your fact-file?

Perhaps you could make some model planets to hang in your classroom.

Questions

1 Which of the planets do you think is the hottest and which the coldest?

2 Do you think that having an atmosphere around a planet might keep it warmer or colder?

3 People often use tricks to help them remember things. You can make up a silly sentence using the first letter of each of the planets like – Mike and Val Eat Moon Jelly Sweets Under the North Pole. Can you think of a way of remembering the order of the planets?

5 Go for a spin!

Do you like roller-coaster rides? What do you like best about them? You might think you are sitting still in your classroom but did you ever think that your classroom, your school and everything on Earth is flying through space at amazing speeds?

The Earth is spinning at 1660 km every hour – that means that in one hour, at the equator, you will be spun through a distance of 1660 km – the distance from Glasgow to Oslo in Norway. Look at how far this is on a globe. Glasgow – Southampton in 15 minutes!

Not only have you travelled that far in a circle but the whole planet is moving around the Sun. In the same hour you have travelled 108,000 km through space. That's like flying nearly four times around the world!

The Earth spins around once a day. That gives us our day and night. When our side of the Earth faces the Sun we get light, when our side is away from the Sun we get night.

Figure 1

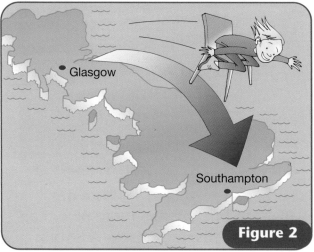

Glasgow

Southampton

Figure 2

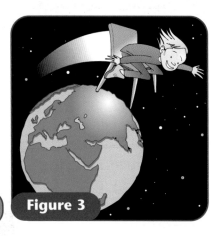

Figure 3

Figure 4

Activity

Try this out with a model of the Earth that you have made. Stick a paper clip into the plasticine to be like a person standing on Earth. Spin your model around and imagine you are the Sun. When the paper clip is facing you they would be in your light. When it is hidden from you they would be in the dark.

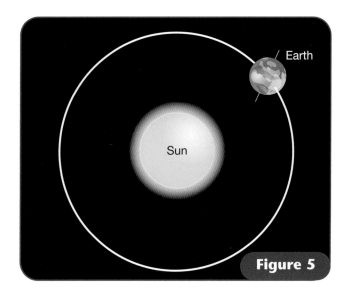

Figure 5

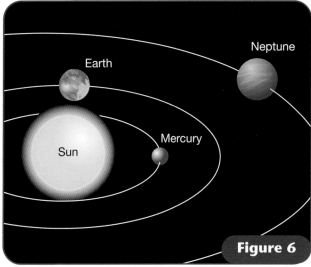

Figure 6

It takes the Earth 365 days to go all the way round the Sun. We call this circle an **orbit**.

All the planets are orbiting the Sun but because some are further away from the Sun it takes them much longer to go round.

Activity

Try this out in the playground or gym. Choose someone to be the Sun at the centre. Now two of you pretend to be planets – one close in like Venus, one further out like Saturn. Both set off together and run at about the same speed. Who gets back to their starting point first? Now try this at different distances from the centre. What do you notice?

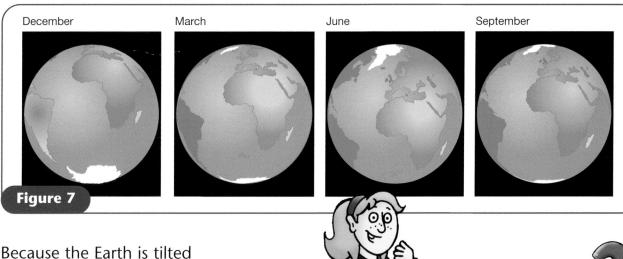

Figure 7

Because the Earth is tilted as it goes around the Sun, light reaching us is sometimes more stretched out than at other times. This gives us our seasons – Winter, Spring, Summer and Autumn.

Questions

1 Why do you think it is warmer in summer and colder in winter?

2 Why doesn't it feel as though you are moving through space?

6 Exploring space

What is space?

Space is the emptiness you see between the stars and planets. Most of the Universe is empty space. The Earth has an atmosphere, a layer of gases that keep us alive. Space begins where the atmosphere ends.

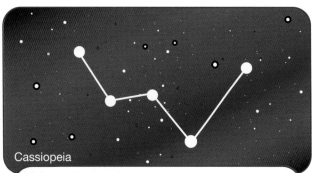

Cassiopeia

Figure 1 Five of the stars of Cassiopeia form a 'W' shape, which forms a clear pattern in the northern sky. It stays in the sky all night long.

How do we explore space?

Ancient people studied stars as long as 3000 years ago. They did this by looking at the night sky. They made careful records.

The telescope was invented about 400 years ago. Galileo discovered sunspots and four of Jupiter's moons.

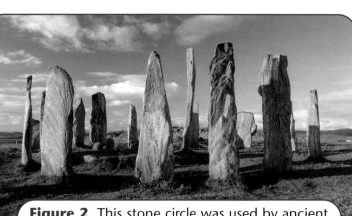

Figure 2 This stone circle was used by ancient people to map the stars and the moon. This helped predict tides, seasons and eclipses.

Figure 3 Galileo's handwritten record looked like this.

Water, dust and street lights can affect what you can see through a telescope. Modern astronomical telescopes are built on the top of high mountains to remove most of those problems.

Figure 4 This one is in the Canary Islands.

Figure 5 This telescope listens to radio waves from space.

Spacecraft

The best way to study the Universe is to get out of the atmosphere. The human race has launched satellites and space stations and has put people into space to continue space exploration.

Most spacecraft do not carry people but are packed with equipment that automatically makes and records things about space.

The International Space Station involves 16 countries. The astronauts who live on board will do experiments to find out about living in space. Everything they need has to be taken up in a rocket from Earth.

Figure 6 The Hubble Space Telescope provides huge amounts of new information on stars and galaxies each day.

Figure 7 This unmanned spacecraft was designed to study Saturn, its rings and satellites (moons).

Figure 8 The International Space Station.

Key ideas

★ Human have always been curious about space

★ Modern scientists use telescopes and satellites to explore space

Introducing materials

If all the world was paper
And all the seas were ink
And all the trees were bread and cheese
What would we have to drink?

Figure 1

Literacy

Material – the stuff that something is made from.

Activity

This funny poem reminds us that we have to use the right stuff to make things. Make a list of five objects that would be no use if the wrong material was used, such as a chocolate teapot!

Using materials

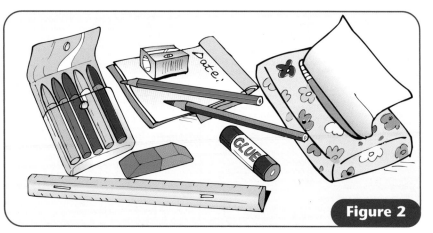

Figure 2

Look at these things.

You might have some of your own. What are they made of? Are they made of the right stuff?

14

What do materials do?

Figure 3

Knives are **strong** and able to **bend** a little. The steel does not easily break because it is **flexible.** Football would be very difficult if the ball would not **bounce** and **squash**. Televisions and other electrical equipment are supplied with copper wires which **conduct** the electricity but the wires must be **insulated** to make them safe. The loudspeakers have **magnets** inside. Fabrics are able to **stretch** over furniture; some feel rough and others feel smooth. The windows are **transparent** – we can see through them – as well as being **waterproof**.

Questions

Look at the picture and make a list of the things materials can do.

1 Choose 5 things in the picture.

2 What are they made from?

3 Why were these materials chosen?

Key ideas

★ Things are made from materials

★ Lots of different materials are used to help us

8 Solids and liquids

Solids

Figure 1

This is where we play. Some of our toys are different **colours**.

A ball is not as **hard** as a stone.

We crashed the truck and now it is a different **shape**.

My bricks can make a neat **stack** but the marbles **roll** all over the place.

I like to **float** my boat. Sometimes I make it **sink** in the bath.

A **magnet** will stick to the frame of the swing. It will stick to the truck but not to the marbles.

I can **squash** the tennis ball but not the marble.

16

Liquids

We have lots of liquids in our kitchen.

Literacy

Liquids are things that spread inside a container and take its shape.

Some liquids are different **colours**. We can see through cooking oil and water but we cannot see through milk.

Oil **feels** very different from water. So does washing-up liquid.

Look at the way the raindrops **stick** on the window. Sometimes they **run** down. The water flows out of the tap. Honey **flows** much more slowly than water.

The oil has spilled and spread over the worktop. Liquids have no fixed **shape**.

Figure 2

Activity

Make a list of the things these materials can do, for example, liquids can be different colours.

When we play in the winter the water has changed into ice and the rain has turned into snow. Liquids change into solids by **freezing**. The ice and snow turn back to water by **melting**.

Key ideas

★ Solids have fixed shapes

★ Liquids flow into the shape of their container

★ Solids and liquids have many properties

★ Some solid materials turn into liquids by melting. Liquid materials can turn solid by freezing

Figure 3

9 Liquids and gases

Liquids

We use all of our senses to detect things. We can **see** through some liquids and they can be different colours. Some **feel** different from others. It is not safe to **taste** a liquid we don't know. Liquids flow from one place to another and they have no fixed shape.

Liquids and gases are both able to flow.

Figure 1

Gases

Gases **move** from place to place. Air is made from gases. The wind is moving air. Some gases are **smelly**!

Gases **spread** throughout the air.

My **floating** balloon was filled with special gas from a cylinder. When I blow up a balloon it **sinks** to the floor.

Gas can be **squeezed** into small places. Try squeezing a rubber ball.

Gas in the kitchen can **burn**.

Liquids and Gases

Liquids cannot be squeezed into smaller places.

> **Literacy**
>
> Liquids cannot be **compressed**, squeezed into smaller spaces.

This allows liquids to be used in many ways.

We have lots of fun with water in the summer! Power blasters squeeze water through the pipes but when air gets into them they stop working. Car brakes work in the same way with a liquid called brake fluid. Some lifts also work with these fluids.

Figure 2

18

Gas can be squeezed, **compressed** into a smaller space.

Soft drinks are made with compressed carbon dioxide gas. A bicycle pump compresses air into cycle tyres.

Figure 3

Changing things

In the summer the water often dries up. Liquids change into gases by **evaporating**. Water is present in the air and it appears on the outside of a glass by **condensing** on its surface.

Key ideas

★ Liquids and gases are able to flow

★ Liquids and gases have many properties

★ Some liquid materials turn into gas by evaporating. Gases can turn into liquid by condensing

Figure 4

Using materials

Using Solids

My house is built from bricks, timber, steel, plastic and paper.

Figure 1

Figure 2

Activity

Look at all the solid things that are in my home and in my bedroom. List the objects and the materials in my house.

20

Using liquids

Figure 3

Figure 4

Figure 5

A lot of our food and drink is liquid. Milk, tea and fizzy drinks are all liquids. They flow freely. Other ones such as yoghurt, ketchup and honey flow much more slowly.

Modern paints contain substances that change into solids in the air. You must always return the top to a tin of paint.

Medicines are often given to us as liquids so that they help us more quickly. We must always take the correct amount of the medicine and use a proper measuring spoon.

Using gases

Gases are used to make drinks fizzy. Some water has natural 'fizz' and others have gas added to them. Gas is also used to spray perfumes, insects or paint. We use gas to blow up tyres and balloons. Some gases prevent things from burning and are used in fire extinguishers.

Figure 6

Questions

1 The home is made from 5 types of material – name two objects that are made from each of them, for example, the floor is made from timber.

2 List 4 solids in the bedroom. Describe the properties they have been selected for that suit them to their job. (A pullover keeps us warm.)

3 Name three uses of gases in the bedroom.

Key ideas

★ We use solid, liquid and gas materials for everything that we do or make

11 The gases of the atmosphere

The atmosphere

We are surrounded by air. The **atmosphere** surrounds the planet with air. We feel the air when the wind blows. We breathe air in and out.

Air is a mixture of gases. Those gases make up the atmosphere. The atmosphere surrounds the Earth. It is a blanket of air, which reaches to 560 kilometres from the surface of the Earth. The blanket is thickest closest to the Earth and gets thinner further away.

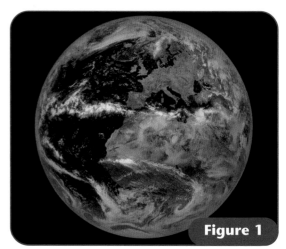

Figure 1

Composition of the atmosphere

There are lots of gases in the air but the main ones are nitrogen, oxygen and argon.

This football crowd represents the gases of the air. Of the 100 supporters 78 have blue hats – they represent nitrogen. How many red oxygen supporters and green argon supporters are present?

The mouse represents the amount of carbon dioxide that is present in 100 parts of air! Tiny isn't it!

Figure 2

Figure 3 Factories like this separate gases from the atmosphere.

Nitrogen

Nitrogen is the big one and makes up most of our atmosphere. You cannot see or smell nitrogen. Nitrogen is not changed easily in chemical reactions – it is generally inert.

Nitrogen is used to freeze food, make fertilisers and chemicals that are important in many industries.

Literacy

Inert means a substance that you cannot easily change.

Oxygen

 Oxygen makes up most of the rest of the atmosphere. All the oxygen in the atmosphere has been made by plants. Plants carry out **photosynthesis** (foto-sin-the-sis) which makes their food as well. We need oxygen for breathing. Oxygen gas allows fuel to burn.

Oxygen is used with other gases to make enough heat to melt steel and **weld** metals together.

Ozone is another form of oxygen. Ozone forms a layer in the atmosphere which shields the Earth from harmful radiation from the Sun. Atmospheric pollution has damaged the ozone layer.

Figure 4

Literacy

Weld means to join two metal surfaces by melting them together

Argon

 Argon is the third major gas in the atmosphere, but only one part in every hundred. Argon also has no colour or smell.

The other gases

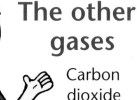 Carbon dioxide makes a tiny amount of the atmosphere. Carbon dioxide is used to make fizzy drinks and fire extinguishers.

Figure 6

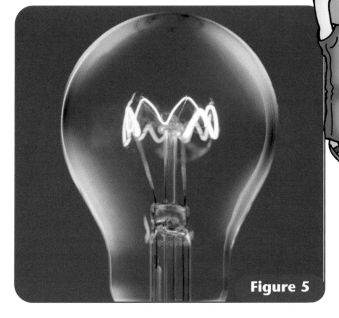

Figure 5

Argon is used for filling light bulbs because it does not burn, or react with other chemicals.

Key ideas

★ The atmosphere is made of gases

★ The three main gases are nitrogen, oxygen and argon

12 Birthday heat!

Figure 1

Figure 2

'This is Past yer eyes milk' Germs in milk are killed by heat – the correct spelling for this is Pasteurised.

 Which of the changes described in the picture are fixed? Which are not?

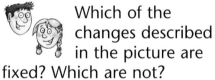 **Activity**

Investigate what might affect making ice in the freezer. What might affect ice cubes melting?

Questions

1 Name two foods that melt when they are heated.

2 Name one food that turns into a solid when heat is added.

3 Name two foods that turn solid when they cool.

4 Name a food that is preserved by freezing.

5 Name two materials that are made by heating and cooling.

Key ideas

★ Materials are changed by heat

★ Some of these changes are permanent, others are not

25

13 Mixing it!

Construction

When we build sandcastles at the seaside we add a little bit of water to help stick the sand together. When the tide comes in there is too much water and our castles wash away.

Figure 1

Figure 2

Figure 3

Figure 4

In olden times buildings were sometimes made of 'wattle-and-daub'– sticks were woven together and the gaps were filled with mud. The roof was often covered with thatch. Ones like these were built on Shetland about 1500 years ago. Modern building methods also include mixtures of materials.

 Concrete is made with different mixtures of cement, sand, gravel and water. Different amounts of these materials are used for different jobs. Large buildings are made with concrete that is made stronger with steel cables.

While the concrete turns hard it also changes chemically. Bubbles of gas are often released and the setting concrete feels warm. Once this has happened the cement, sand, gravel and water cannot be recovered – they have all been changed.

Food

Each time we make a cake we are mixing different materials. The cake can be mixed with spoons or electric mixers.

When you add sugar to your tea, you are mixing materials. Cooking makes many foods easier to eat. The ingredients are all changed when they are cooked. Think about an egg – cooking changes it from runny materials to solid ones.

Figure 5

Figure 6

Figure 7

Kitchen waste can be added

Most of the living things on the compost heap are bacteria

Earthworms and insects live here

Weeds and garden waste can help too

Medicines

 Chemists have mixed materials since ancient times. Herbs and minerals often need to be broken up into powder so that they can be made into medicines. A mortar and pestle is still used in chemist's shops.

Compost

Waste from the kitchen and the garden can be put in a compost heap.

The waste material rots down into useful compost that can be returned to the garden and help new plants to grow. Many tiny animals live in compost – for example, earthworms and tiny insects. But most of the living things – such as bacteria – are too small to see without a powerful microscope. These living things need air and water to make good compost. Gardeners will often mix compost with a garden fork to help add air.

Questions

1 Name two ways to mix foods.

2 Describe how an egg changes when it is cooked.

Some things dissolve in water

Vanishing tricks

 Do you like sugar in your tea? When you stir sugar into your tea it seems to disappear! (It must still be there in the tea because we can taste it.) Salt is the same when we add it to our soup. It seems to disappear but we know that the salt is still there since we can taste it.

Here's what happens.

Salt and sugar both **dissolve** in water. The solid mixes with the water and becomes smaller and smaller. It seems to disappear. The solid and the water make a solution.

Lots of materials dissolve in water – here are some.

Figure 1

Literacy

Dissolve means that the solid becomes part of the liquid. A solution is a mixture of materials.

Figure 2

Some problems

Each of these soluble materials can absorb water and can be spoiled and start to dissolve. They are stored in containers that prevent them from becoming damp – imagine how unpleasant soggy sugar would be! Poster paints would run all over the place and the weedkiller would be much more dangerous! Germs can grow in damp food. Damp materials can become mouldy as well.

Farmers use chemical fertilisers that also dissolve in water. Chemical fertilisers are added to crops to help them grow. If too much fertiliser is added to the fields it will dissolve into the soil, pass into streams and rivers and pollute them.

Some benefits

Most of our blood is water. We need food and oxygen which come from outside our bodies. The blood collects dissolved oxygen in our lungs and carries it around our body. The digestive system dissolves food and carries it round the body.

Figure 3

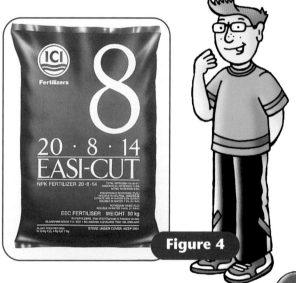

Figure 4

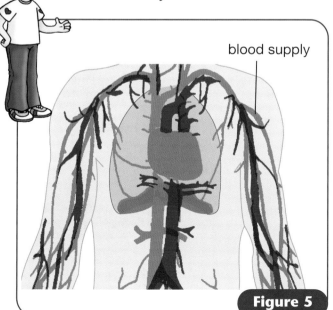

blood supply

Figure 5

Questions

1 Write a sentence that uses each of the following correctly: dissolve; soluble; solution.

2 Why should instant coffee be kept in waterproof containers?

3 How can water damage materials?

4 Which two things are carried around the body in the blood?

Key ideas

★ Lots of things can dissolve in water

★ This can be helpful or it can be harmful

15 Some things do not dissolve in water

Figure 1

 Lots of materials dissolve in water – they are soluble. Many others do not dissolve – they are **insoluble**.

Literacy

Insoluble means that a substance will not dissolve.

Look at each of the containers – they do not dissolve in water – they are insoluble. Plastic, paper, aluminium and glass are all modern materials that are used for packaging food since they are insoluble. This helps to keep the foods pure and they also stop water entering the food and damaging it.

Figure 2

Two thousand years ago the Romans made containers from several materials including glass, pottery, bronze, copper and iron. Each of these could be used to store soluble materials, but they would not dissolve themselves.

Figure 3

A hundred years ago drinks came in bottles like these.

Activity

Make a list of all the kinds of modern containers that carry juice.

Many materials do not dissolve in water

Water comes to our homes through large pipes. The pipes carry water to the kitchen and the bathroom when it is needed. Imagine what would happen if the pipes dissolved! The pipes are made of plastic or metals that do not dissolve in water. The whole water system depends on the water being kept in pipes and special storage lakes called **reservoirs**.

It's teatime again!

Figure 4

Literacy

A **reservoir** is an open water store – often made by damming a river.

Look at what happens when you make a cup of tea. The tea that you drink contains soluble substances – some of these can make you healthier. Other materials do not dissolve – the tea leaves, or tea bags, are thrown away – remember to put them in the compost heap!

Questions

1 Complete each of the sentences using the following words. You can use each word more than once.

Soluble
Dissolves
Insoluble
Solution

Coffee powder _____ in water, but the mug does not. The coffee is _____ and the mug is _____ in water. When sugar is added it seems to disappear – in fact it_____ in water because sugar is _____. The dissolved mixture of coffee, sugar and water is a good example of a _____.

Key ideas

★ Lots of things do not dissolve in water

16 Separating solids

 Sometimes materials are all mixed up and we need to separate them – have you ever lost a toy and cannot find it in the toy box? Wouldn't it be nice if you had a machine to sort them out? People have invented lots of machines that allow them to separate solid materials from each other.

Figure 1

Sieves

Sieves are used in the kitchen to separate solids – tea leaves in the small one, peas in the larger one and pasta in the biggest one. All sorts of sieves are used in machines and factories to separate solid materials.

Figure 2

This machine sieves large stones from the earth to improve growing conditions in the field.

Figure 3

Filters

Sieves that are used for very small particles are called filters.

Figure 4

Tiny coffee particles are removed by the paper filter – it is just like a sieve but the spaces are much smaller – you might look at filter paper through a microscope.

Figure 5

 Why do people sometimes wear masks at work?

Magnets

Substances can be separated from each other if some are magnetic and others are not.

Figure 6

When old cars go to the scrap yard huge magnets can separate magnetic materials from plastic and other waste.

Wind

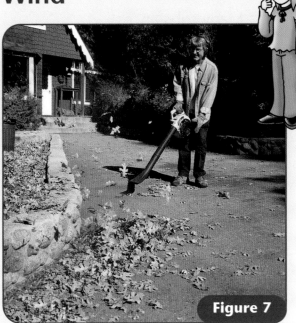

Figure 7

Leaves and other garden waste can be blown away. The leaves are light and can be separated from the lawn using this machine.

Water

Materials that float can be separated from those that sink. Can you think of some?

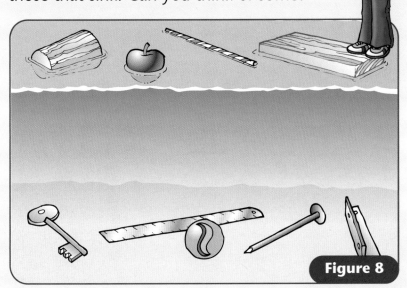

Figure 8

Floating and sinking can be used to separate materials – they can then be recycled.

Activity

Design a machine that would be able to sort all the rubbish from your home.

Key ideas

★ Solids can be separated in several different ways

33

There and back again

Many substances dissolve in water but others do not. Plastic and glass are insoluble. Salt and sugar are soluble in water. We can get the dissolved substances back again by removing the water.

The sea tastes salty. It is a solution of many different types of salt. In hot countries salt is taken from the sea and is used to make table salt.

Figure 1

This salt has been extracted from the Mediterranean Sea in France. Here is how it is done. Sea water is allowed to flood shallow lakes. The sun and wind **evaporate** the water and leave the salt behind.

Literacy

Evaporate means the removal of water by heating which leaves the dry solid.

Figure 2

Activity

Try this experiment.

1 Add three heaped teaspoons of salt to half a cup of water to make a strong salt solution.

2 Stir the solution until all the salt has dissolved.

3 Place three drops of the solution on a clean saucer and leave in a warm, dry place.

4 Find out what happens.

A bit cheesy!

About 30 thousand tonnes of cheese are made in Scotland each year. Solid cheese starts as liquid milk. Remember Miss Muffet? She was the girl that ate 'curds and whey' – these are a mixture of solid and liquid parts but how are they separated?

The curds are the solid parts that become cheese and they are filtered out of the liquid whey. The cheese is pressed to remove the liquid and stored to mature into cheese. The liquid whey still contains useful sugar that can be purified by evaporating the water.

Figure 3

Key ideas

★ Evaporation can be used to get soluble substances back from a solution

Water funny liquid!

During the winter it often becomes so cold that water turns into ice. Ponds and puddles freeze and become slippery. Snow is solid rain. Snowballs can hurt!

DANGER THIN ICE

Figure 1

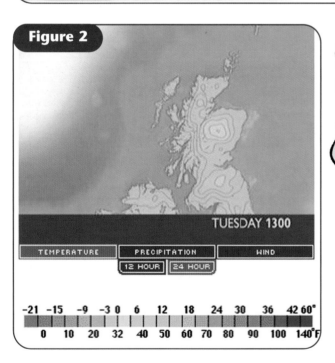

TUESDAY 1300

TEMPERATURE   PRECIPITATION   WIND
12 HOUR 24 HOUR

-21 -15 -9 -3 0 6 12 18 24 30 36 42 60°
0 10 20 32 40 50 60 70 80 90 100 140°F

The blue areas in the weather forecast show where it will be freezing and ice will appear. This happens at temperatures below zero degrees Celsius– and is written as 0°C. Salt is put on to roads and pavements to prevent accidents. Snow might fall and we know that winter has arrived! Water freezes and turns solid during weather that is below 0°C. Water melts at temperatures above 0°C.

The Arctic and Antarctic are places where it is much colder and the sea will freeze.

Figure 3

Freezing is sometimes useful

 We all like ice cream. Ice cream needs to be kept in a freezer so that it stays solid. When you take it out of the freezer it starts to melt and if you leave it out it all turns to liquid. Food is frozen to make it last longer and prevent it from going bad.

Figure 4

Freezing is sometimes harmful

Figure 5

Water gets bigger when it freezes. Ice can break pipes and cause water to leak all over the house. It can be avoided by wrapping the pipes in **insulating** material. **Antifreeze** is added to water in car radiators to prevent damage by freezing.

Figure 6

Hillwalkers and mountain climbers sometimes need to be rescued during the winter. They risk frostbite and hypothermia.

Questions

1 Look at the weather map.
   a   Can you find the temperature where you live?
   b   Where is the coldest area of Scotland?

2 Match the correct clothes for each of the following temperatures:
   20 °C   Shirt and jumper
   0 °C   Tee shirt and shorts
   10 °C   Several layers, hat scarf and gloves

3 What is the freezing temperature of water?

4 What is the melting temperature of water?

Key ideas

★ Water freezes and melts at 0°C, zero degrees Celsius

The greatest hoax

Skull fragments found in 1908 in Piltdown Quarry, Sussex seemed to supply information on human evolution. Scientists thought that they came from a creature that lived a million years ago.

Cro-Magnon man   Piltdown man   Neanderthal man

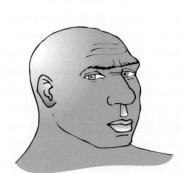
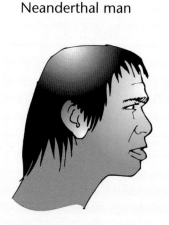

Figure 1

Although some people were doubtful and believed that the remains were from different animals 'Piltown man' seemed to supply the 'missing link' between apes and human beings. By the middle of the twentieth century chemical tests showed that the bones were indeed from different animals and the world of science had been fooled. The new evidence showed it to be a hoax.

Activity

What evidence exists to show that man landed on the moon?

The first moon landings

'**Tranquillity base here, the Eagle has landed.**' These words announced the first landing of human beings on the Moon on 20 July 1969.

Some people believe that the Moon landing never really happened and that the TV pictures were sent from the desert. They are sceptical about the Moon landings. They challenge the evidence that is supplied to support the Moon landings.

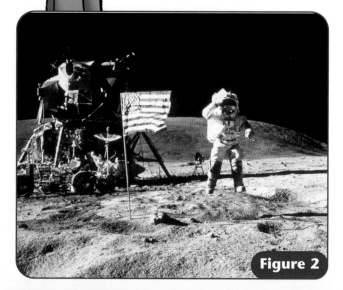

Figure 2

Just an illusion?

In 2003 the illusionist David Blaine spent 44 days without food, living in a transparent box in London, on water only. Or did he? Are you sceptical about this? What evidence exists to show that he really did do this amazing feat or was it just an illusion?

Figure 3

Amateur magic

Try this trick on your family and friends to see if you can fool them.

1 In secret, strap a matchbox with a few matches inside to your wrist.

2 In front of an audience, put two empty matchboxes on the table.

3 Shake each box with different hands so the audience only hears a rattle with one box.

4 Mix up the boxes on the table to confuse the audience.

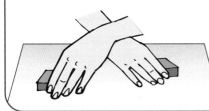

5 Ask the audience to guess which box has the matches inside.

6 They will always be wrong!

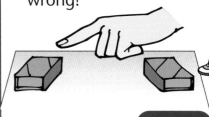

Figure 4

 When you do this trick the audience will doubt whether any matches are present and try to find out how the trick works. They will think scientifically and test their ideas, looking for evidence to support their ideas.

Key ideas

★ We need to examine the evidence that supports scientific facts

★ Being sceptical means that you examine those facts

★ Illusionists can fool us all

39

Gale and Kenneth's puppy is getting wet when it rains. They want to make the puppy a coat to keep her dry but they don't know which type of fabric to use. Mum has several different types so they need to discover which one will be the best to keep out the rain.

Kenneth decides that they will test the fabrics to find out which one to use.

Figure 1

Activity

Can you help Gale and Kenneth to decide which fabric to use?

In your groups see if you can think of a way to test the fabrics to see which one keeps out water the longest.

Figure 2

Gale thinks that one way to try is to put a piece of each fabric over the top of a plastic cup and to hold it in place with an elastic band. If they drop water onto the fabric one drop at a time they could find out how many drops they could put on before the water seeps through into the cup.

Do you think this is a good plan? Is there anything that they will need to think of to make this a fair test?

Should the drops all be put into the same place on the fabric or spotted all around?

Should the dropper touch the fabric or not?

Activity

Try this investigation with some fabric samples. Decide what you are going to do to make sure it is a fair test. Write down your rules.

Before you start, let everyone in your group handle the fabric samples and decide which one is going to keep water out the best and which one will let it through the quickest. Write down what you think.

Write down what happens in a table like this –

Fabric sample	My Guess	How many drops before the water seeped through?
1 – Cotton		
2 – Wool		

Was your guess right?

Was the best material for keeping out the water special in some way?

Milly the puppy likes to roll and play in the rain. What would happen to your best fabric if you rub the water into the fabric?

Repeat your test on dry samples but this time rub the drop of water into the fabric each time. Do your results change?

Gale and Kenneth found a good fabric that was waterproof even when you rubbed it. They made Milly the puppy a coat and she was very pleased!

Did you know?

Charles Macintosh invented many new ways of using chemicals in his Glasgow factories. He is best remembered for inventing waterproof cloth that was used for making coats – we call coats Mackintoshes to this day

Look at some fabrics that have been used to make waterproof coats. What is special about them?

21 It's a beautiful day

What do you notice on a beautiful summer's day? It's warm and bright and there won't be many clouds in the sky. What do you notice at night? It's colder and dark. What makes the difference? The Sun of course!

We get our light and heat from the Sun.

Light and heat energy travel through space from the Sun.

Activity

Investigate what happens when you leave some chocolate in the Sun. How could you stop or slow down the melting? Design and make a box to keep chocolate cool.

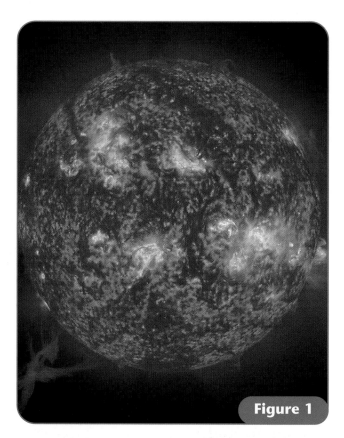

Figure 1

Figure 2

Look at these two pictures. What are the differences between day and night? What special things do we have to use to cope with the heat and light from the Sun?

What special things do we need to use at night to help us cope with the cold and dark? How do animals find their way in the dark? How do they keep warm at night?

What is different now? Is it warmer? Is it lighter? How can you see by the moon?

Activity

Make two drawings of a room in your house to show how different it is during daytime and night-time.

Questions

Why don't we get heat from the Moon?

Figure 3

The Sun is a huge ball of burning hydrogen gas and gives off lots of heat and light. The Moon is made of rock like the Earth but it reflects the light of the Sun back to the Earth. We can often see the Moon during the day too.

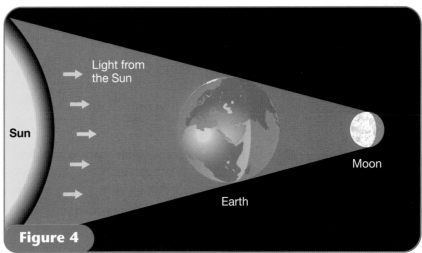

Light from the Sun

Sun

Earth

Moon

Figure 4

Activity

Try this out for yourselves. Take a small spotlight and leave it switched on for a while. Now hold your hands close to it but don't touch. What do you feel? What do you see? Now take a mirror and hold it about 2 metres from the lamp. Move it about and you will see that you can bounce the light from the lamp onto a wall or someone behind the lamp. What do they feel? What do they see?

Dark and silent

Where's the darkest place you know? Can you imagine being alone in a pitch black cave with no torch or lights? What would it be like? What could you see?

1

As she went further into the tunnel, feeling along the cold stone walls, suddenly the floor gave way. Cath found herself falling, bumping off the sides of a twisting downward shaft. Suddenly she fell. Her torch went out with a 'Splat!!' as it hit the ground. She immediately landed on top of it, bruising her knees and chest on the rocky floor. Breathing heavily, she slowly opened her eyes... there was no light, none at all...

What do you think Cath could see?

2

She closed her eyes quickly again – no change – she couldn't see anything – just a total velvet blackness all around. Gingerly she felt around her for the torch – it was useless. The broken pieces lay around her on the cold floor. She held her breath and listened...

What do you think Cath could hear?

3

Nothing... only the sound of her heart racing in her inside as she felt the panic rise...

What would Cath need to be able to see? What would Cath need to be able to hear?

Activity

Get into groups and write down ten things that give out light energy and ten things that give out sound energy. Can you think of a way Cath could make some light?

Can you make a very dark area in your class? Perhaps you could put a black cloth over a table or even look into a dark box. Can you see anything if there is no light? Let a tiny bit of light into your dark space – can you see anything now?

Our eyes are very sensitive to light – we can't see anything without light, but even if there is just a tiny bit of light, we can start to make out the shapes of things.

When it is dark and there is only a little light, do you see in colour or in black and white?

Discuss this with your group and try it out in your dark area.

4

Cath fumbled in her pockets – nothing ... no matches, no lighter, no torch, nothing. Alone, bruised and sore, despair swept over her. She started to sob. The walls of the cave echoed her cries as though there was someone else there. Shocked at the sound she fell silent again and huddled further into herself ...

Why do you think her cries sounded so loud? What do you hear when you sing in the bath? Why does it sound different to singing outside?

5

Suddenly she heard a distant noise – Ranjiv! 'Cath' he called.

'I'm here' she shouted. 'I've fallen but I'm OK. Do you have a torch?'

'Yes, I'm coming down, hold on!'

Suddenly the cave was filled with sound 'Arghhhhh' and Ranjiv arrived through the hole in the roof and fell on top of her.'

Before Ranjiv fell down the shaft, she could hear Ranjiv but she couldn't see the light from his torch. Why not?

Activity

Talk about this in your groups. Try it out in your classroom. If someone stands outside the room, behind the wall and shines a torch at the wall and shouts 'Hello', can you hear them inside? Can you see the light from their torch?

What have you found out about light and sound?

45

Ranjiv and Cath are still in the cave. Help is on its way because their friend Sonja heard Ranjiv fall and ran back out to raise the alarm. Neither of them is hurt but they can't reach the hole in the roof to climb out.

 Light travels in straight lines so things close to a light source stop most of the light from reaching any further. When things are further from the light, they only stop a small part of the light.

Activity

In your groups, write down a few things you know about shadows. In a darkened room, try doing the same as Cath – make shadows on a screen and see how they change when you are close to the light and away form the light. Can you see why the shadows change?

1

Ranjiv's torch survived the fall and shone brightly around the cave. 'We might have to wait for ages until they reach us with a rope,' he said to Cath. She looked glum so he tried to distract her by making animal shapes with his hands in front of the torch. She laughed as a huge, crazy-looking rabbit shadow hopped across the wall of the cave. 'Let me try!' she said and held her hands close in front of the light. The shadow on the wall was huge and fuzzy. She moved her hands away from the torch and the shadow became clearer but smaller. She moved over to the wall of the cave and the shadow was sharp and the same size as her hands.

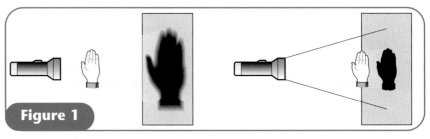

Figure 1

2

Cath and Ranjiv started to play with the shadows from the torch making fantastic shapes moving and writhing across the cave wall. Suddenly, Cath noticed that her shirt was making a shadow on the wall but it was not as dark as the one her hands made. She tried other things in front of the torch and found that their shadows were different shades of grey. Ranjiv noticed what she was doing and tried some coloured tissues his mum had given him. The pink tissue made a pink shadow, the green one a green shadow. Now they could make coloured shapes on the wall.

Activity

Try this out for yourself. Find some materials that you can see through – clear plastic, cling-film, poly-pockets, tissue paper. Compare the shadows they make when you hold them in front of the light. Try some coloured tissue paper. What do you see? Now look through the things you have tried. What can you see through them? What do you notice about what you can see and what sort of shadow they make?

When we can see through things fairly clearly they make a very pale shadow. We say they are **transparent**.

Some things absorb all the light and make dark shadows. We cannot see through them at all. We call them **opaque**.

Some materials absorb some of the light – we cannot see through them clearly and can only make out colours or large shapes and they make a darker shadow. We call these **translucent**.

3

Ranjiv looked carefully at the beam of light from his torch. "Light must travel in straight lines if you think about it," he said. "Look how the beam of my torch looks like a cone of light – you can see the edges of it and they're straight."

"Is that why I couldn't see the light from your torch when you were up in the tunnel and yet I could hear your voice?" asked Cath.

"Sound must be different," said Ranjiv and went quiet while he thought about it.

What do you think? Get together with a group and pool your ideas.

24 Bouncing around

Ranjiv and Cath are still in the cave. They are playing with Ranjiv's torch while they wait to be rescued.

1

'If your torch only gives out a narrow beam of light, why can I see other things in the cave outside of that beam?' asked Cath.

'I don't know,' replied Ranjiv. 'The light seems to be bouncing off this wall and lighting up the rest of the cave.'

'Try bouncing it off the other wall,' said Cath. Ranjiv turned the torch onto the other wall – it was darker stone and suddenly the whole cave seemed darker. 'Quick, point it back to this wall. That one makes everything seem spooky!'

said Cath. Ranjiv turned the torch back to the first wall and then tried moving it about all over the cave. In some places the cave seemed to get brighter and in others it got darker. The rock walls of the cave were different colours and in some places the surface was shiny with water.

Activity

Try this out in your groups. Use a tube made from a piece of rolled up black sugar paper and put it onto different coloured surfaces and look down it. Can you see some colours better than others? Try it on different types of surface – rough or smooth – does it make a difference? Try it on a mirror – what do you see now? How could Cath and Ranjiv get the best light in the cave? Which surface would give them the most light?

2

'Look at my white trainers – they're very bright when I shine the torch on them,' said Ranjiv.

'Try this special strip on mine – Wow, it looks like it's lit up inside,' said Cath. 'My Mum said that's called a reflective strip – it's there so I can be seen in the dark when I'm out!'

'I've got a strip like that on my jacket,' said Ranjiv and he turned the torch onto the sleeve of his jacket. The special strip shone brightly in the gloom.

Figure 1

Activity

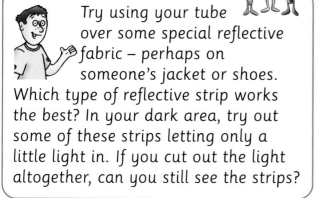

Try using your tube over some special reflective fabric – perhaps on someone's jacket or shoes. Which type of reflective strip works the best? In your dark area, try out some of these strips letting only a little light in. If you cut out the light altogether, can you still see the strips?

Light is reflected or bounced off surfaces. Some surfaces absorb the light – dark colours absorb more than light ones, rough absorbs more than smooth. Reflective strips are made from tiny crystal spheres that reflect the light very well.

Activity

From what you have learned about reflecting light, make a picture of two people walking along a road at night – choose colours to show one person wearing very reflective clothes and the other wearing dark clothes. Who do you think would be seen the best by a lorry or car travelling along the road?

Carry out a survey of the jackets worn by children in the class. Which ones would help their owners to be seen at night and which ones wouldn't? What could you do to make sure you can be seen?

 Ranjiv and Cath are still in the cave but their torch is growing dim. They hope the rescue will come soon.

 1

The two children sat quietly as the torchlight slowly faded. As the last remaining glow went out they huddled together. Cath started to hum her favourite pop song and Ranjiv joined in. "It's funny how your lips tickle when you hum isn't it?" said Cath.

"See if you put your hands on your throat when you're talking, you can feel it moving" replied Ranjiv.

"There's such an echo in here", said Cath. "Everything sounds louder and sort of odd."

"Listen to this then" said Ranjiv and pulled an elastic band out of his pocket. He pretended to play it like a guitar – stretching it and relaxing it to make different sounds. "I can feel this vibrating to make the sound. Here you try." He passed the elastic band over to Cath. She played with the band plucking it harder to try to hear the sound it made. Soon she plucked so hard the band snapped with a ping and flew out of her hands to be lost in the darkness. "Drat" she said.

Activity

Do what Cath and Ranjiv did – try placing your hand on your throat and sing a few notes. What can you feel? Watch some rice on a drum skin – what happens when you gently tap the drum?

Figure 1

 Sound is a sort of vibration that our ears can detect and our brains translate this as sounds.

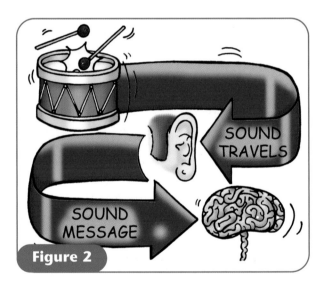

SOUND TRAVELS

SOUND MESSAGE

Figure 2

Activity

Try out their experiments with an elastic band. What happens when you pluck harder? What happens when you stretch the band tighter and play?

Bigger vibrations make louder sounds, faster vibrations make higher sounds.

2

"Listen Cath, can you hear something?"

Cath listened hard "There's someone coming!"

Soon the sounds got louder and the children could hear people's voices and the clanking of metal.

Suddenly the cave was filled with the sound of their names being called and they quickly shouted back, telling their rescuers that they were okay but couldn't get out. Within a few minutes they could see faint flickering lights through the hole in the roof. They shouted in their excitement and the noise echoing round the cave was deafening.

A single voice shouted down – "Listen a minute. We're here to get you out, but the hole's too small for us to get through. We need to use a drill to make the hole bigger – some rocks have fallen in. It's going to be very loud. Cover your ears with anything you can find and stay away from the hole!"

Ranjiv and Cath grabbed their jumpers and coats and bunched them up around their ears as the shrill note of a drill filled the cave with a deafening scream.

Activity

Can you find materials that absorb sound – make things seem quieter? Could you design a 'quiet hat' – one that keeps out as much sound as possible? Who could use one of these?

Just like some materials absorb light, some materials absorb sound.

3

The rescuers lifted the children through the hole and out of the cave. They were dazzled by the bright lights outside and were hugged and scolded by their anxious parents. The muddled sounds of people talking seemed loud and confusing after the quiet of the cave and they were glad when they were finally taken home to bed after promising never ever to go exploring like that again!

Get switched on!

Figure 1

Activity

How many things in the picture need electricity to work? If there was a power cut which things would still work? What could the family use to allow them to see in the dark?

In groups, make a list of all the things in the picture that use electricity. Look at your list and circle things that use mains electricity in red and things that use batteries in blue.

Most electrical things use mains electricity but some work from batteries.

A battery is like a tin of stored energy – once you use it up you have to put more in by recharging it or recycle it and buy a new one.

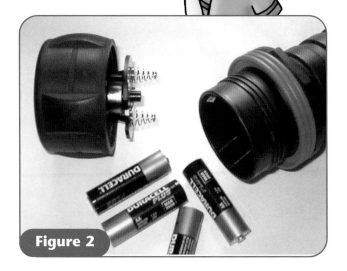

Figure 2

To make things work, electricity has to flow around a loop called a circuit. For a torch to work the bulb needs to get electrical energy from a battery. The energy is carried to the bulb by electrons. For a buzzer to sound it needs electrical energy from the battery.

Activity

Use the items you have to make some simple circuits. If you have a buzzer make this circuit.

What happens if you take one wire off? What happens if you swap the wires over so that the red wire goes to the negative end? What could you say about your circuit from this?

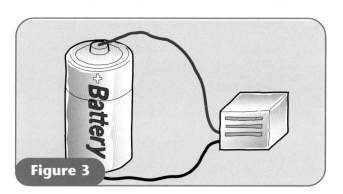
Figure 3

The electrical energy the electrons carry is changed to sound energy in the buzzer. The electrons must return to the battery to collect some more. This means they travel in a loop called a circuit. If the circuit is broken anywhere then the electricity will not flow and the buzzer will not sound.

Some electrical things need the electricity to flow in a certain direction for them to work.

Now try using a motor like this.

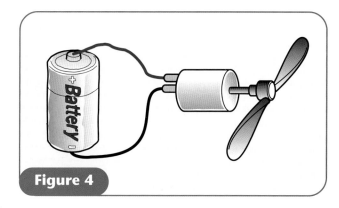
Figure 4

 We can make circuits with other things – try using a bulb and two wires like this to make a light. Does it matter which way round the wires go this time?

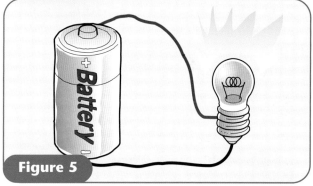
Figure 5

Activity

 In groups, draw a large picture of a helicopter and make up the circuits above. Cut a hole for the bulb to go through to make a headlight for the helicopter, put the motor behind the picture so that the propeller turns at the top of your picture and have the buzzer behind to make the noise.

53

To light or not to light

This is a gadget that used to be used for sending messages before telephones were invented. A circuit was made using a buzzer and a way of turning it on and off so that a series of beeps could be sent along a wire. The beeps were given special meanings – one long beep meant the letter 't', two short beeps followed by one long one and another short one meant the letter 'f'. By using a tapper to make the buzzer work, messages could be sent many miles through wires that were carried on poles – a huge circuit!

Figure 1

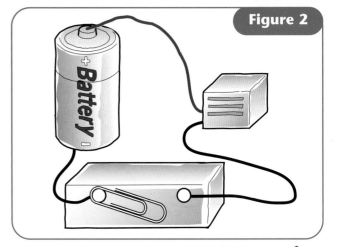

Figure 2

Activity

Can you make a circuit with a buzzer and make long and short beeps by taking one of the wires on and off a terminal?

To make this easier we could make a switch. Do this using a block of plasticine and two drawing pins.

Wrap a wire around each of the pins as you see in the picture, then slide a paper clip over one of the pins. You can now uses the paper clip to touch the other pin by sliding it across. What happens when the paper clip is touching both pins?

Literacy

A **terminal** is a point where you can connect a wire.

You have made a switch. Why does the buzzer sound when both pins are touched by the paper clip? Can you send a message to one of your friends using morse code?

The switch works because electricity can flow along the paper clip and so complete the circuit.

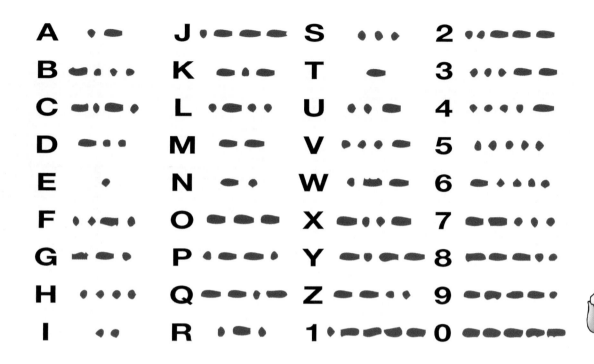

A	•–	J	•––––	S	•••	2	••–––
B	–•••	K	–•–	T	–	3	•••––
C	–•–•	L	•–••	U	••–	4	••••–
D	–••	M	––	V	•••–	5	•••••
E	•	N	–•	W	•––	6	–••••
F	••–•	O	–––	X	–••–	7	––•••
G	––•	P	•––•	Y	–•––	8	–––••
H	••••	Q	––•–	Z	––••	9	––––•
I	••	R	•–•	1	•––––	0	–––––

Figure 3 Tap out the international distress signal SOS.

Activity

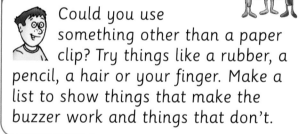

Could you use something other than a paper clip? Try things like a rubber, a pencil, a hair or your finger. Make a list to show things that make the buzzer work and things that don't.

Literacy

Materials that let electricity pass are called **conductors**. Things that won't let electricity pass are called **insulators**.

Activity

Can you send a **silent** message to someone in another room or across the classroom using Morse code?

Lighthouses are used to warn ships at sea of dangerous rocks. They flash a strong beam of light in a special pattern that identifies that lighthouse. Can you make a lighthouse and make up your own special pattern of flashes for it? Lighthouses can also make a very loud sound to warn ships of the dangerous rocks when there is thick fog. Could you put a buzzer into your lighthouse and make up a sound code for it?

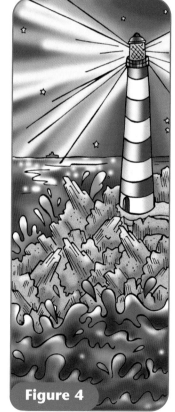

Figure 4

This is Professor Rozi. She has built a machine that will make perfect pizzas in just 5 minutes. She has a problem – she wants to see if it works by plugging it into the mains electricity but she knows that metal conducts electricity. She thinks that if she plugs her machine into the socket, she might get an electric shock. What do you think?

What could she do to her machine to make it safe? Think of the things you have that use mains electricity. What do they have covering them to make them safe?

Can you draw her machine once it has been made safe? Put labels on your picture to show the materials you would use.

Electrical things need conductors to carry the electricity and insulators to protect us from it. Insulators keep us safe. Most electrical things we use have lots of metal parts inside them but are covered in a plastic case to make them safe. The pictures show a TV with and without its plastic case. What materials can you see inside and outside the TV set?

Figure 1

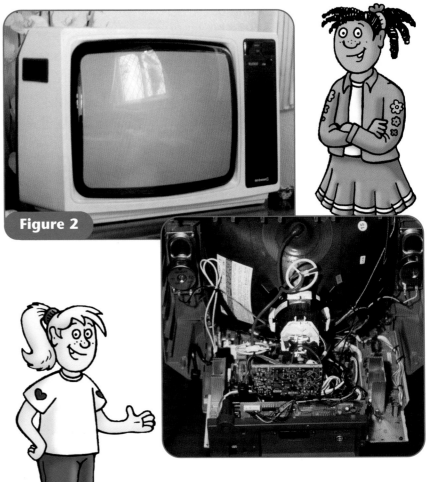

Figure 2

Your body is a good conductor of mains electricity; but mains electricity is deadly. We have to make sure that we use electricity carefully. There are some simple rules that Professor Rozi will tell you about.

Be safe with electricity

Figure 3

1 Never touch bare wires.

2 Switch things off before you plug them in or unplug them.

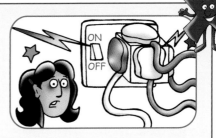

3 Don't have too many things plugged into one socket.

4 Never run cables under the carpet – they get worn and can catch fire.

5 Never touch anything electrical with wet hands or get electrical things wet.

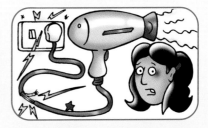

6 Don't use things that are damaged or cracked.

Activity

In a group or with a friend, look at the room that has lots of electrical things. Some of them are not safe to use. Make a list of the dangerous things you can see. Can you think of anything in your own house that breaks the safety rules?

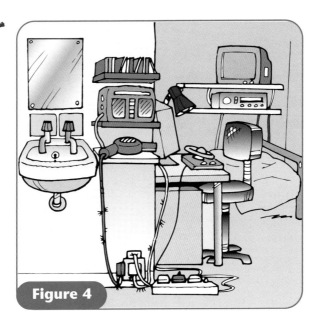

Figure 4

Can you design a machine that uses electricity to do something? How could you make sure it is safe to use? Draw your machine and label the conductors and insulators on it.

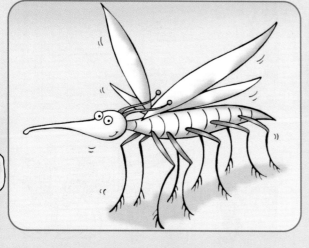

This is a jitterbug. The jitter bug never seems to stop moving.

It flies about all the time, zig-zagging around being a real nuisance.

This is a lazybug. It does as little as possible.

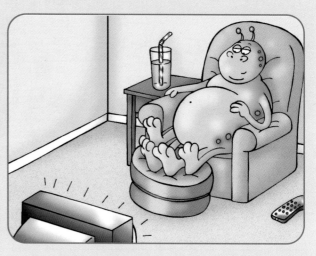

The lazybug just sits around all the time. It doesn't move unless it has to.

Which bug uses lots of energy? We call this being energetic.

Literacy

Energy is the stuff that makes things happen. We need energy to move, to grow and to think.

Activity

Draw some things the bugs might do in their day – the jitterbug might ride a bicycle or run a race, the lazybug might sleep or play on a computer or read a book.

Write down some of the things you do during the day. Draw a circle around the ones that are energetic.

The jitterbug has stopped flying about. He's run out of energy.

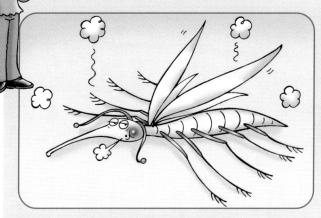

What do you think he needs? Where can he get more energy?

We get our energy from food. Food is stored energy and our bodies can take in food and use it for growing, thinking, moving and keeping warm.

Some foods give us more energy than others. Do you know of any 'energy foods'? Look at the ones shown below. Which ones do you think have the most energy?

Some high-energy foods give us the wrong sort of energy – they get stored as fat unless we are very active. Other foods don't give us much energy but have good things like vitamins in them that keep us healthy.

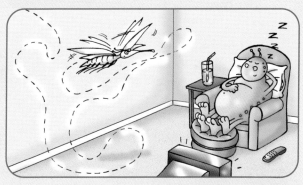

What will happen to the jitterbug if he keeps eating but stops taking exercise?

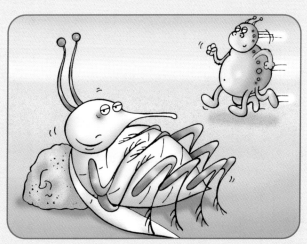

Energy is what makes things happen. Without energy, nothing can change. Energy is never made or lost but it is always changed from one type to another.

If we visit the energy swap shop we can see how this can happen. Kenneth has stored energy from the food he has eaten. In the swap shop he can change that into movement energy to let him run about but he also gets some heat energy which makes him warm and warms up the air around him.

Figure 1

Figure 2

Figure 3

Carrie is a carrot plant. She takes some light energy from the Sun and exchanges it for some chemical energy to make her grow and some stored energy. She stores the energy in her leaves and roots – it makes the carrots that we take and eat.

Freddy is a fire, he takes stored energy from sticks, wood, coal and gas and changes it into light, heat and sound energy.

Figure 4

Activity

Work in groups and see if you can decide which energy exchanges will happen for these characters –

1 Pollyanna wants to sing in the choir at school. She takes in some stored energy from the food she has eaten.

2 Rana is a wind-up radio, what sort of energy does she take in and give out?

3 Yuri is a yo-yo that is wound up.

4 Solly is a calculator that works off a solar cell.

Look at the cartoon strip below and see if you can decide which energy exchanges are happening in each picture.

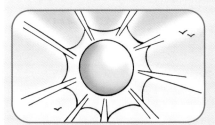

Gases burn in the Sun.

Plants use light to make food to grow and make seeds.

Animals eat the plants for food.

Animals use the food to grow and to make their babies.

We eat food from plants and animals.

We move, make noises and heat.

WATTS WONDERFUL ELECTRICAL STORE

Figure 1

This is another type of swap shop. All the things in here need to use electricity which is a type of stored energy.

Activity

Make a list of all the things you can see in the shop. Now opposite each one write down what it changes the electrical energy into. The first one is done for you here:

heat
movement
and sound

washing
machine

Activity

Electrical energy changes into several different types of energy in some items, for example, a TV produces heat, light and sound.

Now talk about your list with the other people in your group. Do they agree with you? Do you need to change some of your answers?

You might have noticed that heat is in all your entries. All energy changes produce some heat energy.

A computer gives off lots of heat – it might have a fan inside to cool it down. The monitor gets hot too. All of this heat is wasted energy.

Figure 2

An ordinary light bulb gives off lots of heat. Have you ever put your hand near a reading lamp when it has been on for a while?

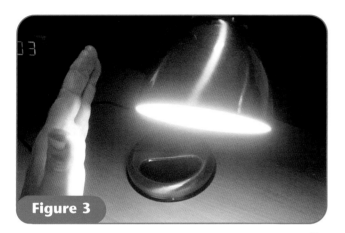

Figure 3

All the wasted heat energy gets lost into the atmosphere and out into space – it is lost to our Earth. Fortunately, our Sun produces lots of heat and this replaces the energy we lose.

The amount of energy we lose as heat lets us know how well something is working. We call it efficiency.

Literacy

Efficiency means comparing how much you get out of something with how much you put in.

We say that something is working very efficiently when there is little energy wasted in producing heat. For example, an energy efficient bulb, produces the same amount of light as an ordinary bulb but much less heat. That means it uses less electrical energy.

Figure 4 We use 'Watts' to measure electrical power. The ordinary bulb uses 100 Watts of electrical power each hour to produce light and lots of heat. The energy efficient bulb produces the same amount of light, but only uses 20 watts in an hour because it produces much less heat.

 Most big electrical items such as fridges and washing machines now carry an energy efficiency rating on the front when you buy them. 'A' means very efficient – very little energy wasted, 'F' means not very efficient – a lot of energy wasted.

Try to find out how much these two washing machines would cost to run for 10 minutes if 1 kwatt costs 5p.

A type A washing machine uses 1 kilowatt to run for 1 hour.

A type D washing machine uses 5 kilowatts to run for 1 hour.

Which machine would be more expensive to run? Which is more efficient?

When we want to move something from one place to another we can either push it or pull it.

Figure 1

Pushing things

When you push a football it starts to move. A kick is really a hard push. The harder you push a ball the faster it moves.

A football can be kicked in lots of directions during a game. The ball goes from end to end and side to side depending on the direction that people kick it.

Every time a football is kicked something else happens –you can see that it has changed shape.

Figure 2

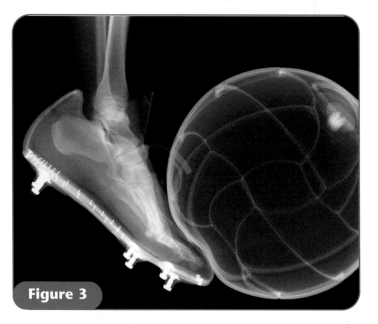
Figure 3

When an object is pushed three things can happen – it can change direction, speed or shape.

Pulling things

We can also pull things but this has the same result as pushing them.

Figure 4

Figure 5

The breakdown truck is pulling the car back to the garage. The harder it pulls the faster they go. When the driver turns the steering wheel they will travel in a different direction.

This tool pulls on the dent in the car body and changes its shape.

Things that push and pull are called **forces**.

Questions

1 Describe what will happen to the spaceship in terms of direction, speed and shape when each of the following things happen:

   a The pilot fires the rocket at 1

   b The pilot fires the rocket at 2

   c The asteroid collides with the spaceship

Key ideas

★ Pushing or pulling something changes its direction, speed or shape

Magic magnets

What is magnetism?

Magnetism is a force that pulls some materials, like paper clips or a nail, towards a magnet.

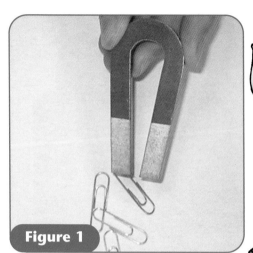

Figure 1

Different kinds of magnetism?

Ancient people found magnetic stones that they called 'lodestones' because they pointed in a north direction. These were used as compasses by ancient people like the Vikings.

Orienteering is a popular sport that depends on reading a map and using a magnetic compass. A compass always points north and south because the Earth is like a great big magnet.

North

Figure 2

Figure 3

Figure 4

Special materials make permanent magnets. Other materials become magnetic when they have electricity passed through them.

This electromagnet is strong enough to lift cars – when the electricity is switched off the car is dropped by the crane.

Where are magnets?

We use a surprising number of magnets in our homes. The fridge door is closed with a magnetic strip. Decorative fridge

Figure 5

magnets are used to leave messages on the door. Did you know that the pump at the back of the fridge has powerful magnets that drive the electric motor?

All electric motors must have magnets inside them to make them work. A DVD player has magnets inside the motor that turn the DVD inside the machine. Its loudspeakers have magnets inside them as well. Video and audio tapes use magnetic materials.

Computer disks also work magnetically. Look at some credit cards – they also have magnetic material on them.

Figure 6

Hospitals use magnets for lots of purposes, for example, removing metal objects from our bodies. Modern hospitals have MRI machines that even allow us to look inside the body by using magnetism.

Figure 7

Magnetism makes this experimental Japanese 'Maglev' train float above the track. It can travel at more than 552 kilometres an hour. It would take this train less than an hour to travel from Edinburgh to London!

Figure 8

Activity

Can you find any other magnetic items in your home?

Use a compass to find magnetic materials.

Find out more about the 'maglev' train.

Questions

1 Name two different kinds of magnets.

2 Describe two ways that magnets are used in hospitals.

3 List five ways that we use magnetic materials.

4 Is the Earth magnetic?

Key ideas

★ Magnetism is a force that pulls magnetic materials

★ There are different kinds of magnets

★ Magnets are used for many things including electric motors and compasses

34 Magnetic!

Which materials are magnetic?

Activity

Use a bar magnet to find out which type of materials are magnetic and which sorts are not.

I think that metals are magnetic.

Things that are not metals are not magnetic.

I think that some metals are magnetic.

What do you think? See what you can find out.

Magnets and directions

A compass is a bar magnet that is used to help us find our directions. The end that always points towards the North Pole of the Earth is called the North Pole of the magnet. The other end, called the South Pole, seeks the opposite

Activity

What does it feel like when you bring bar magnets together the same way as these pictures?

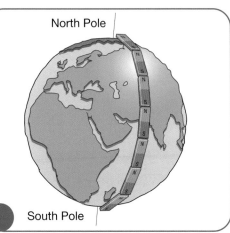

North Pole

South Pole

Figure 1

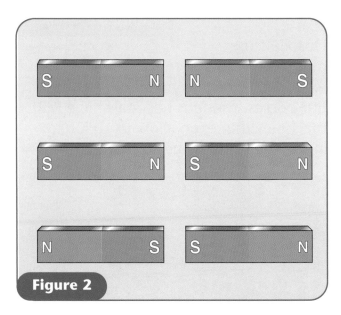

Figure 2

The Law of Magnetic Poles

The laws of magnetic poles say that similar magnetic poles repel and opposite magnetic poles attract.

This means that when you try to put two north poles or two south poles of magnets together they will push apart – they repel each other. When you bring the north and south poles of different bar magnets together they will pull together – they attract each other.

The strengths of magnets

Some magnets are weak and others are very strong. Sometimes they are so strong that they are difficult to separate. Imagine trying to open the fridge if the magnetic seal was too strong! Here is how you can test the strength of magnets.

Figure 3

Pass thin sheets of different magnetic and non-magnetic materials into the space between the paper clip and the magnet and see what happens.

What do you think will happen?

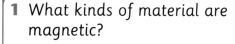
Questions

1 What kinds of material are magnetic?

2 What kinds of materials are non-magnetic?

3 Describe what happens to magnets when you bring them together using the terms: magnetic poles, attract and repel.

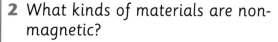
Key ideas

★ Magnetism is a force that pulls magnetic materials

★ Only some materials are magnetic

★ A bar magnet always points towards the North and South Poles of the Earth

★ Similar magnetic poles repel and opposite magnetic poles attract

69

The gang are having a day out. They have found a great park to play in.

Activity

Make a list of all the things you can see the children doing in the picture.

Now imagine you were at the park today when it is icy. Look at your list of activities. Circle the activities you could not do on an icy day because they would be dangerous. Are there any that might be better? Circle these in a different colour.

What is it that makes the difference?

Figure 1

Figure 2

Some surfaces grip and others don't. Think about the floors in your house or school. Which surfaces grip and which let you slide a little?

Activity

Why are some surfaces slippery and others sticky? In your groups talk about your ideas and see if you can decide what is happening when you slip or grip on a surface.

This bike has bumpy tyres so that it can grip between the stones on the ground.

The bike has big tyres so your weight is spread more and holds the bike on the ground.

These children are talking about their ideas. Do you agree with any of them?

When one surface rubs against another, there is a **force** that tries to stop them moving. That force is called **friction**.

The knobbly tyres get sticky as you go along and stick the bike to the ground.

Friction is a force that tries to stop things moving. Rub your finger along the desk and then along a carpet or a similar rough surface. Which was the easiest?

The desk, which is smooth, is a low friction surface. The carpet, which is rough, is a high friction surface.

When you rub your finger to and fro on a surface like your desk (not too hard or you will hurt your finger!) – your finger gets hot. Friction always produces heat. When we are cold, we rub our skin to make it warm – it is friction from your hand rubbing your skin that makes the heat.

Now look back at the picture of the gang in the park. Which surfaces can you see that are high friction surfaces? Which surfaces are low friction surfaces? What sort of things can you do to change a surface from low to high?

Figure 3

Activity

Investigate some low friction and high friction surfaces using some boxes that have surfaces of different materials – smooth card, carpet, sandpaper etc. Try pushing or pulling them along the desk with a forcemeter.

Literacy

A **forcemeter** looks like a spring balance but measures in units of force called Newtons rather than in grams.

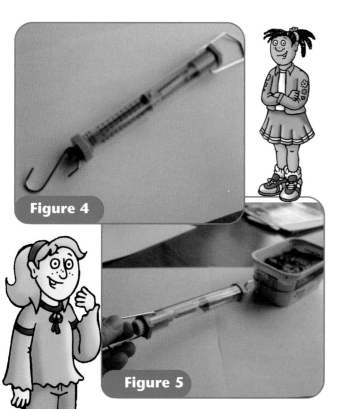

Figure 4

Figure 5

What did you discover? Try putting some plasticine inside the boxes to make them heavier. Remember to always use the same amount of plasticine to make it a fair test.

What did you discover this time? Are your answers different to your first investigation?

What would happen if you did the same investigation on a rougher surface? Do you think you would get different results if you did the investigation on ice?

Look back at the children with the bike. Do you think that large surfaces have higher friction than smaller ones? How could you find out?

36 Shudder and slide

Get a grip

We use friction for all sorts of things. If you tie a bow with your shoelaces, it stays done up because friction between the two strands stops them from coming apart. If you have very smooth shoelaces then they will come undone easily.

Figure 1

If there was no friction, how would you manage to pick up a cup or glass or hold a burger?

When you play football, it is friction that allows you to run. If you fall and skid along the ground, you might get a friction burn – your skin gets burnt by the heat of friction against the ground.

Figure 2

Figure 3

Activity

Can you draw a pair of pictures to show friction or not friction –

1 for three cars parked on a slope

2 for some children ice skating?

Smoothly does it

Sometimes we need to reduce friction for something to work. Think about a bicycle – if there was a lot of friction between the parts that turn the wheel, then it would be difficult to move on it.

Skiers wouldn't get far if there was a lot of friction between their skis and the ground.

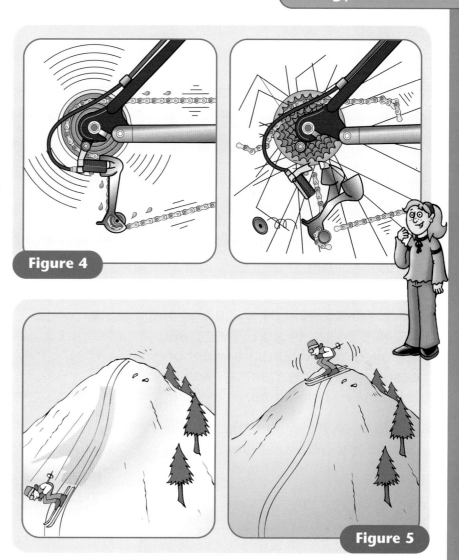

Figure 4

Figure 5

Activity

Can you think of some ways we can reduce friction? In groups make a list of some things that need to have low friction for them to work. Look at your list. What is it that reduces friction in that system?

Figure 6

Can you design a shove-halfpenny game to test these liquids for slipperiness?

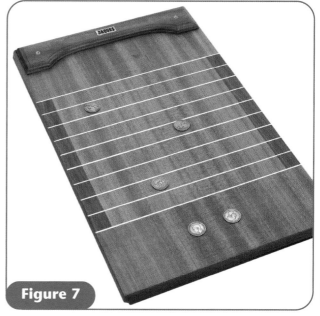

Figure 7

We have looked at friction between solids, now we are going to think about friction in other ways.

Splash

Think how it feels to be running on land and then think how it feels if you try to run when you are in the swimming pool, up to your chest in water.

Figure 1

Imagine trying to run through peanut butter. What would be stopping you? Friction is trying to stop you moving. If there were no friction, the water or peanut butter would simply slide past your body and you would move easily through.

Do you think it would make a difference if your body were a different shape?

Figure 2

Activity

 In groups, talk about this problem. How can you move easily through water? Think about the different shape you make in the water when you swim.

Try dropping a 50p piece into a cup of water. If you let it go so it lies flat on the surface before sinking, does it fall to the bottom faster or slower than if you let it go it end-on to the water? What does this tell you about moving through water?

What does it feel like if you jump into the water in a pencil shape? Have you jumped in with your arms and legs spread out? Sometimes this can hurt. Divers try to enter the water in a pencil shape with their arms above their head. If they get this wrong it is called a belly-flop and gives them sore legs and arms where friction burns them as they enter the water.

Figure 3

OW!!!

Swimmers who swim in international competitions like the Olympics now wear special suits that allow the water to pass over their bodies more easily. Making less friction means they go faster.

Figure 4

Figure 5

Float

Have you ever seen a film of people jumping out of an aeroplane sky diving? Sometimes they 'lie down' as they fall before they open their parachutes. This slows them down. Can you guess why?

If they want to fall faster they aim their bodies towards Earth like a diver entering the water. This speeds up their fall. Once they reach a certain height they must open their parachute to slow them down or they will crash into the ground.

Activity

Why does a parachute slow the skydiver down? Do you think the size and shape of the parachute is important? Can you make a simple parachute out of plastic cut from a carrier bag and attached at the corners by some string or sewing thread? Does the parachute work if there is no weight hanging from it? Use some plasticine as a weight and try dropping your parachute from different heights. Try changing the shape of your parachute or change the weight at the bottom. What do you notice? Can you make the best 'chute – the one that slows down a given weight of plasticine the most?

Friction is our friend and enemy. We use friction to stop our cars – the brakes rubbing on the wheels makes them stop. Friction from air resistance slows the car and makes it use more fuel.

Figure 1

Things moving through air are slowed down by the friction of the air against them. If we make things smoother and a better shape, we can cut down the friction. We call this streamlining.

Modern cars are designed to slip easily through the air. They have no handles sticking out and all the surfaces are smooth and curved in a way that allows the air to slip over them.

Activity

In your group make a list of some other things that are streamlined to slip through the air.

Easy does it!

You can feel how much resistance there is by making two paddles from the lid of a margarine tub. Make one flat and the other folded in a V shape. Try pulling each one through a box of sand.

Now try pulling the paddles through a bowl of water.

Figure 2

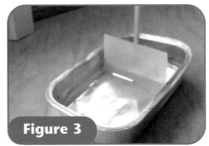

Figure 3

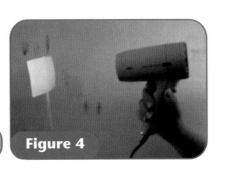

Figure 4

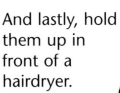

And lastly, hold them up in front of a hairdryer.

Speed merchants

Animals are streamlined too.

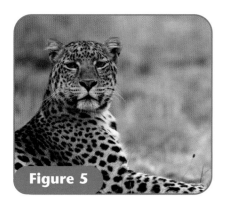

Figure 5

These animals have smooth skin or feather surfaces and their bodies are graceful curves that allow them to move quickly on land, in the sea and in the air.

Many sports people now wear clothes that are designed to be aerodynamic.

Literacy

Aerodynamic means that something has a very good shape and surface texture to allow air to slip past it easily – a low-friction surface.

Activity

 Look at the pictures of sports people below and decide how each one is streamlined to make them go faster.

Most modern passenger planes are a good shape to travel fast – they travel at about 925 k.p.h. (kilometres per hour). Back in 1960 a new shape of plane was designed and built to carry passengers even faster – it travelled faster than the speed that sound travels at – over 2178 k.p.h.! It was called Concorde and for over 30 years carried passengers around the world at **supersonic** speeds. It could do this because of its special shape, surfaces and huge jet engines. Concorde is no longer in service because the planes became too old and expensive to run.

Figure 6

 Can you make a paper aeroplane that looks like Concorde? Can you make it fly? How could you make it fly even better?

Great scientists who have walked on Scotland's streets

James Watt figured out how to make the steam engine faster, more efficient and safer while he was walking on Glasgow Green. Steam engines powered factories and trains – these helped transport and industry throughout the world.

Thomas Graham discovered dialysis – the technique that is used in hospitals throughout the world to purify patients' blood when they have kidney disease.

Sir James Black won the Nobel Prize for Medicine in 1988. This is awarded to the world's greatest scientists. He attended Beath High School in Fife.

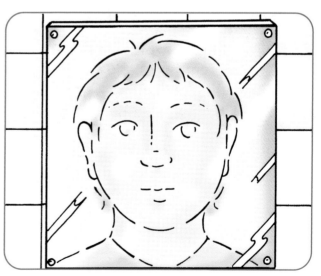

This person might make great discoveries about the Earth, space, energy, forces or living things. They might simply enjoy learning about science. Is this person you?

Blow, bow, bang, twang!

Figure 1

Kenneth needs an instrument to play in the Hashem Bashem Band. He has some glass jars that he can use. He is going to put water into the jars to make different sounds when he taps them with a pencil.

He is going to investigate how to make different notes and sounds using his jars and pencil.

What things might make a difference to the sound he makes? In your groups make a list of things you could change.

Remember for this to be a fair test you can only change one thing at a time, so if, for example, you change the shape of the jar, you have to keep the amount of water you use the same.

Figure 2

Investigate the sounds you can make with this simple set-up. Can you tune your jars to match the notes on some chime bars or on the piano?

How can you make the note higher? How could you make it lower?

Can you write some instructions for someone who wants to make a set of jars to play a tune? What should they make sure about the shape of their jars? How much water should they use for each note?

Practise with your set of jars until you can play a tune. If some people in your group make other instruments you could learn a tune together and play it for the rest of your class.

You could make some pipes using straws of different lengths. When you blow across the top of the straws you will make a sound. What happens when the straw is shorter or longer?

Is this like the water in the jars?

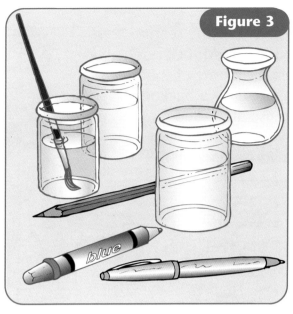

Figure 3

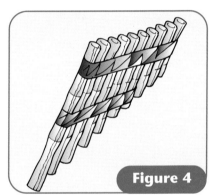

Figure 4

You can make a reed instrument from straws by taking a straw and cutting the end into a point.

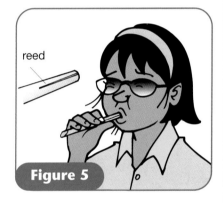

Figure 5

Blow gently through the cut end to make a different sound.

You can make a string instrument by using a plastic or paper cup and cutting slits in it and a hole in the bottom. Thread a piece of string through the hole and tie a large knot so that it won't pull out. Tie another large knot at the bottom and wipe some candle wax down the string. Now if you pull your fingers down the string quickly, you'll make a different sound. It sounds a bit like a cockerel crowing. Make a cardboard cut-out cockerel to fit into the slot.

Can you say something about things that make high notes and things that make low notes from your investigation?

 # Our day at the seashore

We went to the seaside and collected rock pool animals. Some of them do not have a backbone – these are called **invertebrates** (in-vert-e-bray-tes).

Figure 1

Some of the animals have shells. The animal's soft body is found inside the shell. A limpet's mouth scrapes food from the surface of rocks, while mussels filter food from sea water. They are all sensitive to light and often have eyes on the ends of stalks.

Some of the animals have hard outer skeletons – they are a bit like suits of armour that knights wore in the olden times. They have lots of pairs of legs. They also have sensitive eyes and 'feelers'. Crabs and lobsters have strong pincers to help eat their **prey**.

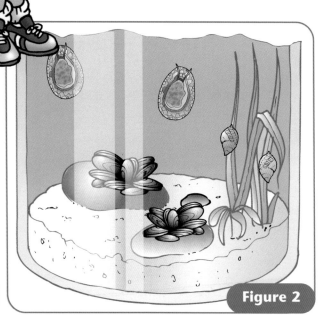

Figure 2

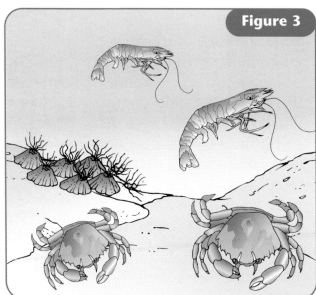

Figure 3

Jellyfish and sea anemones have **tentacles** – be careful these can sting you! The tentacles help to pass food to their mouths. Jellyfish and sea anemones are both very similar and although the sea anemones are stuck to the rocks – they are really like little jellyfish that have been turned upside down!

Starfish have five arms. These have powerful suckers beneath them that help them move on the seashore and prevent them being washed away by the waves. Sea urchins and starfish live on the sea bottom – some are **predators** and others are **scavengers**.

Figure 4

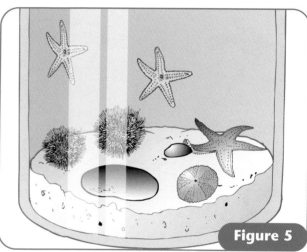

Figure 5

Literacy

Invertebrates are animals without backbones.

Prey are animals that are eaten by **predators**.

Tentacles are long soft arms that surround the mouth of jellyfish.

Questions

1 What is the name of the group of animals that do not have backbones?

2 Name one thing that each of these animals have in common.

Limpets and mussels
Barnacles and crabs
Jellyfish and sea anemones
Starfish and sea urchins

3 Now name one thing that is different about each of these pairs of animals.

Activity

Find out more about one of the groups that the children found in their rock pool.

Key ideas

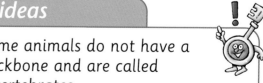

★ Some animals do not have a backbone and are called invertebrates

★ Many different kinds of invertebrates are found in rock pools

We went to the countryside and collected invertebrates. Animals without backbones are called **invertebrates**.

Figure 1

Some of the animals are **insects**. These always have three pairs of legs – six in all.

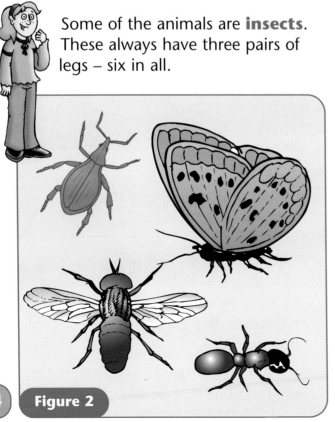

Spiders always have eight legs – four pairs. Many spiders make webs to trap their prey. Their bite can help to kill the prey as well as start to digest it!

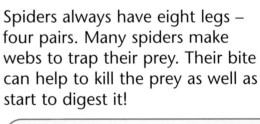

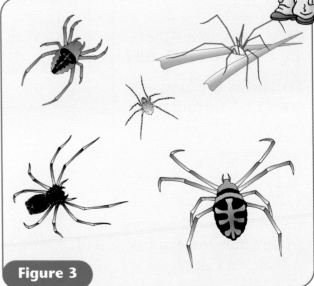

Figure 2

Figure 3

Some animals have even more legs. Slaters have seven pairs. It is very difficult to count the number of legs on centipedes and millipedes. We found these ones under rotting leaves and wood.

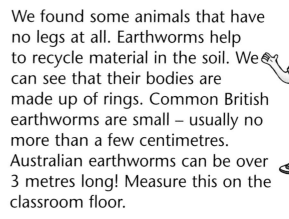

We found some animals that have no legs at all. Earthworms help to recycle material in the soil. We can see that their bodies are made up of rings. Common British earthworms are small – usually no more than a few centimetres. Australian earthworms can be over 3 metres long! Measure this on the classroom floor.

Slugs are really like snails that have lost their shells. Their bodies have no rings at all. Snails and slugs are related to the mussels, periwinkles and limpets that we found at the seaside.

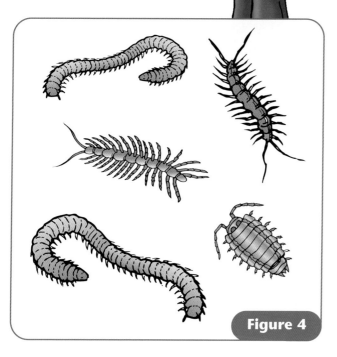

Figure 4

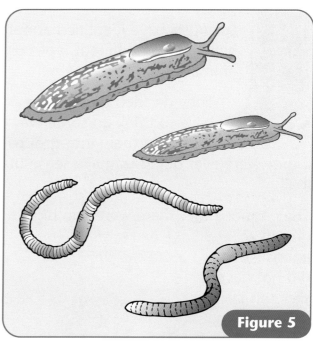

Figure 5

Literacy

Invertebrates are animals without backbones.

Questions

1 Name one thing that each of these animals have in common.

   Ant and butterfly
   Money spider and harvestman
   Slaters and centipedes
   Earthworms and slugs

2 Now name one thing that is different about each of those pairs of animals.

Activity

Find out more about one of the groups that the children found in the moorland.

Lots of different animals are vertebrates, so the scientists divided them into five groups. Let's look at some of them.

Look at your list of animals. Draw a circle around all the ones that have bones inside.

Splash

The first group is the **fish**. What do you know about fish?

Activity

How many animals can you think of? Work with your group to see how many you can write down.

Scientists have identified about half a million different types of animals.

They decided they would have to think up some way of sorting them into groups if they were ever going to make sense of it all.

They noticed that there were two big groups – animals that did not have a skeleton inside and those that did – so they chose this to start.

Can you feel your bones? What do they do in your body? How would you manage without them?

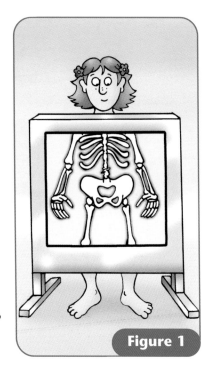

Figure 1

Figure 2

Activity

In groups, write down everything you know about fish and then make a list of all the ones you can name. Now look at the picture at the top of page 87 and see if you got some of the things in the boxes.

Its body is the same temperature as the water. We call this cold-blooded.

Has scaly skin.

Some fishes like sharks and rays, have a flexible skeleton and can grow replacement teeth.

Lays soft eggs in water and doesn't usually look after its young.

Have gills that allow them to breathe in water.

Figure 3

Hop

Figure 4

Here's a creature that you might find in your garden. He has moist skin – it feels smooth and damp to the touch. He breathes air now but when he was very young, just hatched out of his jelly-egg, he was able to breathe water like a fish because he had gills. Gradually as he grew legs and became more like a frog, he grew lungs inside his body and his gills disappeared. He feels cool because his body doesn't make any heat. Instead he sits in the Sun for a little while until he warms up and then hops off to catch some grubs. He's a member of the group we call **amphibians**.

Literacy

Amphibians are a group of animals that are able to breathe through both their skin and their lungs and so can live in water or on land.

Newts are in that group too.

Figure 5

Activity

Make a model fish and a model frog for your classroom and use cocktail sticks to put labels on your models to show the things you have learnt about them. (Bubble wrap marked with a felt pen dot makes great frog spawn).

44 *Scales, feathers and hair*

Figure 3

They lay eggs that have a tough leathery shell.

Scales

Our next group has lots of members that you will know. The **reptiles** include all these animals. Let's look and see what they have in common.

The young look like tiny adults when they hatch but most struggle to survive and get no help from mum or dad.

Figure 1

Feathers

Figure 4

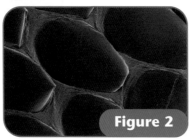

Reptiles all have scaly skin but it is dry to the touch.

Figure 2

Where do these birds live?

They all breathe air but do not make any heat for themselves – they are all cold-blooded and have to sunbathe before they can become active.

Birds make a huge group. They come in all sorts of colours, shapes and sizes. They make all sorts of noises – some can even make sounds like a phone or someone talking. They have made homes everywhere on the planet.

Can you decide what the features of birds are?

Think about these things – skin, eggs, parents, warm or cold?

Figure 5

The last group is also very big – so big that we are in it too!

Hair

Figure 6

We call the group we are in the **mammals**.

Mammals all have things in common.

We all produce heat inside our bodies – we are warm-blooded.

Figure 7

We have hair on our skin.

Figure 8

We give birth to live babies not eggs.

We produce milk to feed the babies.

Figure 9

Activity

Which groups do you think these animals belong to? Talk it over in your groups and compare your answers with the rest of the class.

1 kangaroo   **2** ostrich

3 salamander   **4** eel

5 alligator   **6** whale

89

Leaves fall from **deciduous** trees in Autumn. Have you ever looked carefully at the leaves?

 How are they the same? How are they different?

Literacy

Deciduous trees lose their leaves in the Autumn. **Evergreen** trees keep their leaves all year round.

Figure 1

Both leaves are green. They have stalks that attach them to the trees.

They are heart shaped. Look at the jaggy edge.

This one has a wavy edge. The base of the leaf is shaped like a triangle.

Figure 2

Activity

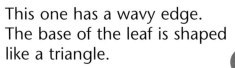 See if you can make a collection of leaves. Press them and stick them on to a piece of paper. Perhaps you can scan them on to a computer. How many differences can you find?

Using a key

More than 1500 tree species grow in Britain but only a tiny number, 32, have always been here.

Scientists use books of pictures and words to identify living things. They are called **keys**.

Literacy

Keys are used to identify living things.

Literacy

A **compound** leaf is made of smaller leaflets.

Activity

This key can be used to identify the four leaves by matching the descriptions to the pictures.

Look at the leaves

Choose the best description

Follow the line to the next description

Name it when you reach the end.

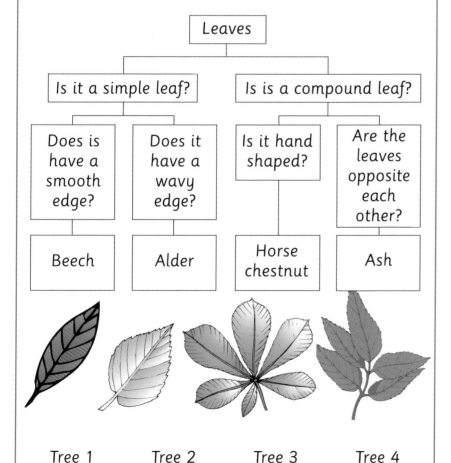

Tree 1   Tree 2   Tree 3   Tree 4

Activity

What else can you say about your leaf collection? So far we have looked at our leaves. What other senses could we use? Elm leaves **feel** rough. Fir leaves **smell** like grapefruit. Rosemary leaves have a strong **taste**.

Safety

Remember do not taste your leaves – they might poison you!

Key ideas

★ Leaves can be different in many ways – we need to observe them carefully to name them

91

Five facts about flowering plants

Fact 1

Flowering plants make seeds. The seeds of flowering plants are completely enclosed inside the fruit.

Some flowers are bright and showy. These often release perfume to attract insects which carry pollen from one flower to another.

Figure 3

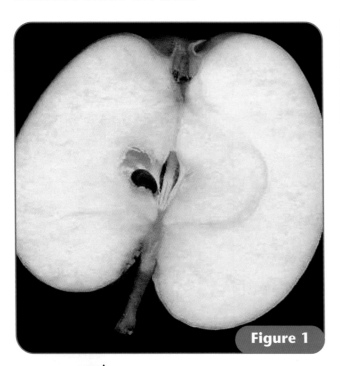

Figure 1

Other flowers are quite dull to look at – their pollen is carried by the wind.

Look very carefully at the apple. Can you see some of the parts of its flower?

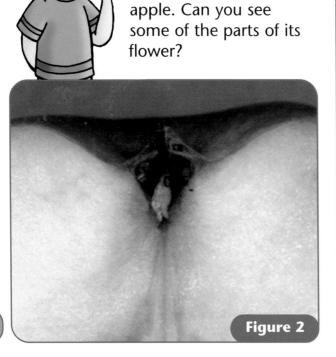

Figure 2

Figure 4

Fact 2

Some flowering plant leaves have parallel veins and others are net-veined.

Figure 5

Fact 3

Flowering plants can be as big as an oak tree or as tiny as duckweed.

An oak tree can survive for as much as 400 years and measure as much as 9 metres all the way around. Duckweed can double every few days. Each plant measures 0.5 cm.

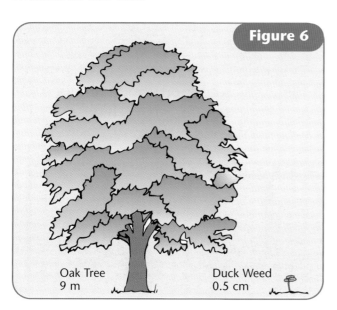

Figure 6

Oak Tree
9 m

Duck Weed
0.5 cm

Fact 4

Flowering plants live in water, and on land.

Some of them survive in very wet places and others live in very dry places.

Figure 7

Fact 5

Figure 8

And finally … Flowering plants have flowers!

Flowers take part in reproduction. Although many different kinds of flowers exist they all need pollen to be carried to the female part of the flower to make new plant seeds.

Key ideas

★ Flowering plants make seeds

★ Flowering plants have parallel or net-veined leaves

★ Flowering plants exist in all sizes

★ Flowering plants live in water or on land

★ Flowering plants have flowers!

47 Non-flowering plants

Have you noticed that many plants do not have flowers? Some reproduce by making spores. Others reproduce with seeds which carry the plants to new places. Lots of different non-flowering plants exist.

Spores spread these plants from place to place. The spores are shaken or fall into the air from the plants.

Figure 2

Figure 1 These are spores on a leaf.

Pine seeds provide important food for birds. They can pick the seeds from between hard scales. Pine seeds are carried through the air by the wind.

Algae

Algae live in water – the sea, fresh water and damp places on land. Some algae are found floating in the water and others are attached to the bottom of the sea or lake.

Algae start the food chain. They make about one third of all the Earth's food which supports huge numbers of living things. Algae are used for many things – fertilisers, surgical dressings and even food.

Moss

Mosses form a spongy mat which helps to absorb and keep water.

Each little plant has a small stem with tiny leaf-like parts attached to them.

Large areas of Scotland are covered with peat. This has been formed by a moss called **sphagnum** (pronounced Sfag-num). This moss was used by Vikings instead of toilet paper!

Horsetails

Horesetails live in lochs and damp gardens. The have straight, hollow stems which seem to fit together like Lego pieces.

Horsetail stems feel quite sharp. Before scouring pads were invented people used them to clean pots and pans.

Ferns

Ferns grow in damp, shady places. Ferns grow directly from the ground and have long feathery leaves.

Conifers

Trees such as pine, larch, spruce and yew are **conifers**. Instead of flowers, they produce cones which contain seeds.

Conifer leaves are needle-shaped. They are usually evergreen. They keep their leaves all the year round.

Key ideas

★ Non-flowering plants reproduce with spores or seeds

★ Algae, moss, horsetails, ferns and conifers are all non-flowering plants

The meaning of life (1)

Nearly a million different plants and animals live on this planet. They look different and live in different places. Have you ever wondered how we know that they are alive?

Scientists agree that all living things have seven characteristics in common.

Characteristic 1

Life is highly organised.

Inside the body	Outside the body

Living things are made from a few simple chemicals – sugar, protein, salt, fat and DNA.

Cells are found inside every living thing.

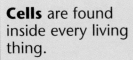

Tissues are cells that look the same and do the same thing e.g. muscle or nerve cells.

Organs are where more than one tissue work together inside the body, e.g. the brain or the heart.

Systems are groups of organs that work together, e.g. the nervous system or the digestive system.

Populations are all the members of the same species living in the same area.

Communities are all the species that are found in the same area, e.g. populations of people, birds and squirrels.

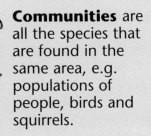

Ecosystems are all the species in one area that depend on each other and are affected by the local conditions, e.g. temperature and water.

The **Biosphere** is all living things and their ecosystems.

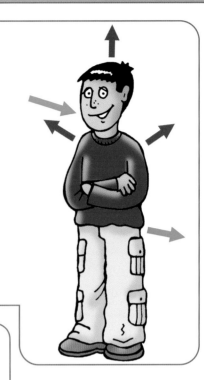

Characteristic 2

Living things exchange energy and materials with the environment

Energy allows living things to work.

Some living things get their energy from light, e.g. plants and algae. Others get their energy from chemical food, e.g. animals and fungi. All living things produce waste. Imagine the mess that would be left if that wasn't removed by other living things!

Scavengers are animals that live on waste materials – think of the gulls that live at rubbish tips.

Characteristic 3

Living things are well balanced

Here is what you are made of – mostly water, salt and sugar!

The conditions inside your body are always the same because your body is balanced. The balance is controlled by your brain and many other parts of your body.

If we feel too hot then we sweat to lose heat. If we lose too much water when we are hot then we feel thirsty and drink to replace it. If the amount of sugar in our blood drops then we eat to boost the sugar level.

If the balance in your body changes you feel ill. When you have a fever it is because your temperature has gone up to fight an infection. Some people's bodies cannot control the level of sugar in their blood. They suffer from diabetes (die-a-beet-is).

All processes in living things are balanced.

WEIGHT 50kg

BODY TEMP 37°c

3/4 volume of body 37.5 litres

Questions

1 Find out about each of the following:

a Parasites	d Fever
b Scavengers	e Hypothermia
c Diabetes	f Isotonic drinks

Key ideas

* ★ Living things have seven things in common – here are three:
* ★ Life is highly organised
* ★ Living things exchange energy and materials with the environment
* ★ Living things are well balanced

Characteristic 4

Responding to the environment

Living things are able to **detect** and **respond** to the environment. Here are some of the ways that you do it.

I can see light, when it is too bright I look away.

I can taste salt – if food is too salty I spit it out.

I can feel heat – when things are too hot I move away.

I can hear sound – if things are too loud I will cover my ears.

Have you noticed that swallows spend the summer here and geese arrive in the winter? These birds migrate to and from different parts of the world. This helps them to avoid poor conditions, to get food and to reproduce.

Plants are also able to detect and respond to the environment. Trees lose their leaves in the autumn. House plants turn their leaves towards the window so that they can get light energy.

Characteristic 5

Living things reproduce

People did not always believe that you need living things to make new living things. The ancient Egyptians believed that maggots came from old bandages rather than coming from flies.

All living things come from parents.

Living things can reproduce by **cloning**.

Mum grew this plant on the window sill by taking a cutting from another one. Most house plants are produced by taking cuttings. Cuttings are identical to the each other and the parent.

Huge greenhouses are used to produce clones of house plants which make our homes more attractive.

Some invertebrates can increase their numbers by simply splitting in half.

Dolly was cloned near Edinburgh. She was the first mammal in the world to be cloned. Cloning is controversial. Some people are very worried about it.

Living things also reproduce by **sexual reproduction**. Sexual reproduction always involves two parents to produce their young.

Characteristic 6

Living things develop and grow

Babies grow inside the mother's womb. Look at some of your old baby clothes and see how much you have grown already! All living things grow and mature.

Sunflowers are very different from their seeds yet each one can germinate and grow into a new complete plant with its own flowers.

Many animals look much the same throughout their lives – you look like small adult humans in most ways – but think how different a butterfly is from a caterpillar. Compare a housefly to its maggot. Look at the beetle and its grub.

Characteristic 7

Living things show adaptation

Literacy

Adaptation means the ways living things are suited to where they live.

For example, an owl is adapted as a night time predator. It has very soft feathers so that its flight is silent; large eyes to help see in poor light and sharps talons and beak to kill and eat its prey.

The thistle is adapted so it not very tasty to grazing animals and the prickles make it nasty to eat. It stands tall in the light and its seeds are high in the air to catch the wind and travel to new places.

All living things show adaptation to where they live.

Questions

1 Which part of your body detects these?

   a light **b** heat **c** sound **d** taste

2 SETL is the Search for Extra Terrestrial Life. How will scientists know that something from outer space is living?

Key ideas

★ Living things have seven things in common – here are four:

★ Responding to the environment

★ Living things reproduce

★ Living things develop and grow

★ Living things show adaptation

99

Can you imagine what you would be like if you did not have any bones? Would you be able to move?

We need our bones to give us our shape, to protect some of our insides and to allow us to move.

Let's look at the bones in our body.

Figure 1

Our bones are hard and strong. In children they are still growing. They grow from the ends. They can mend themselves if they get broken but have to be put back into place before they heal to make sure they mend the right way.

Activity

See how many of your bones you can feel and name. Write a list of the bones you find. How many do you think there are?

Shape

We call the bones in our body a skeleton. Your **skeleton** makes you the shape and size you are. It also protects some parts of you. Which parts of your body are protected by bones?

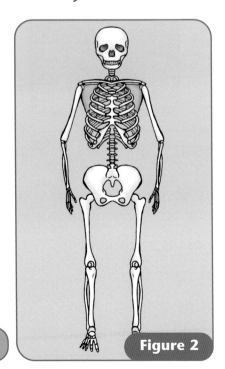

Figure 2

Figure 3

Protection

Your brain is protected by your skull.

Your heart and lungs are very important parts of your body and they are protected by your ribs.

Your spinal cord is very important too – it runs down your back inside your backbone and carries messages between your brain and the rest of your body.

Movement

Your skeleton allows you to move.
You have lots of muscles – these are special soft parts that can pull themselves

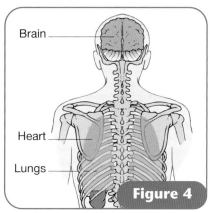

Brain

Heart

Lungs

Figure 4

up to become short and tight or relax to become long and thin. They can be very powerful.

If the ends of the muscle are stuck onto two different bones, then when the muscle pulls tight – we say it **contracts** – it moves the bones.

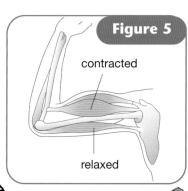

Figure 5

contracted

relaxed

Literacy

When something gets smaller we say it **contracts**.

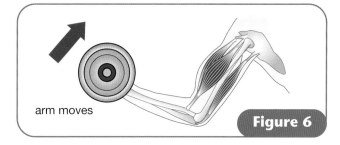

arm moves

Figure 6

Try it for yourself – hold the muscle in the upper part of your arm and use it to lift the lower part of your arm up.

Figure 7

All your muscles work this way. To give you all the movements you need the muscles work in pairs – as one contracts, the other relaxes. Now do the same movement with your arm but this time hold the back of your upper arm – can you feel the muscle there moving opposite to your biceps muscle?

The muscles need two things to work – food in the form of a sugar called glucose and oxygen. They get both of these from blood. As muscles work they make waste materials – water and carbon dioxide. Both of these are taken away by the blood.

Activity

Try moving different parts of your body and feeling for the pairs of muscles working. How many pairs can you find?

Feel the joints in your body – the places where two or more bones meet. Are they all the same? Can you move some parts of your body differently to others? Write a list of the types of movement you can do with different joints.

Squish, squash, gurgle, pop!

Squish

We all eat every day. What happens to the food we put into our mouths? We are going to find out. Let's think of your **digestive system** being like a machine in a factory.

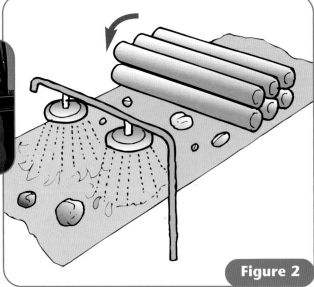

Figure 2

Literacy

The **digestive system** is what we call the parts of your insides that deal with the food we eat.

First of all we put food into our mouths. What's inside there? Sharp **teeth** that cut, smash and grind up the food.

Activity

How many teeth have you got? Are they all the same? Use a dental mirror to look at your friend's teeth and count them. Can you and your friend decide what each type of tooth does to the food you eat? Write down what you think.

Liquid is added to the food to help mash it up. Once it is squashed enough, it travels down the **gullet** in small chunks.

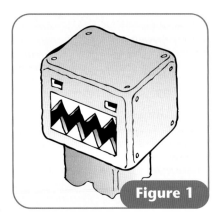

Figure 1

Squash

At the bottom, it drops into the **stomach** where the smashing and squashing carries on. Here lots of a strong liquid mixed with acid is added that kills off nearly all of the nasty germs that might have come in with the food. Still, you must always wash your hands before handling or eating food.

Gurgle

The food stays in your stomach for a long time – about 5 hours. Once it is all mixed and sludgy it is let out, a bit at a time, from the bottom of the stomach into a very long tube called the **small intestine**. This tube is zigzagged inside you to fit it all in. If it were opened out it would be about 8 metres long! Inside this tube, more liquid is added to help break down the food into its basic bits – proteins, carbohydrates, fats and sugars.

Where have you seen these words before?

The food (now in liquid form) is sucked out through the wall of the intestine into the bloodstream where your body can use it. The parts of the food that your body cannot use are called waste.

The small intestine is joined onto the **large intestine**. Here water that was put into the food to mash it up, is taken back into the bloodstream.

Figure 3

Pop

At the end of the large intestine the waste is stored to be released when you go to the toilet.

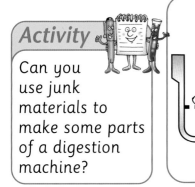

Activity

Can you use junk materials to make some parts of a digestion machine?

Figure 4

With water going into the blood whenever food and drink are digested, we also have to get rid of it when our blood becomes too thin. This happens in our **kidneys**. These are found on each side of your body at the back.

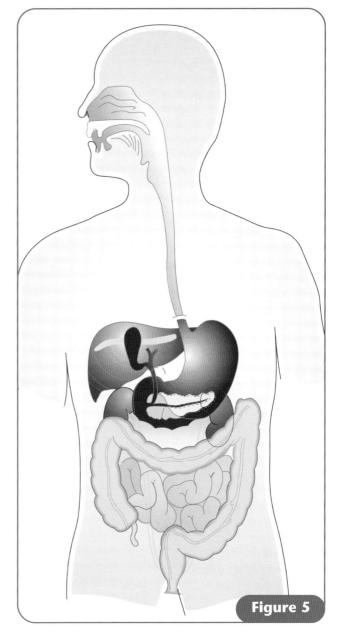

Figure 5

The kidneys act like a filter taking out the extra water and some waste things from your blood. This all empties down tubes called **ureters** into your **bladder** that stores it until you can go to the toilet.

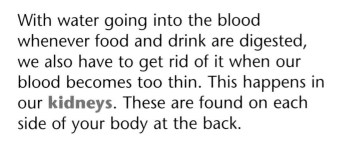

Literacy

The **ureter** is a tube that goes from the kidney to the bladder.

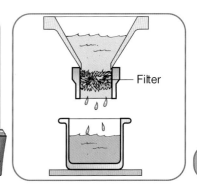

Filter

 Whoosh, phew, swish, boom!

Whoosh

What are the two ways we decide if someone is alive? Yes – we look for breathing and listen for a heartbeat. What happens when we breathe? What is our heart doing when it makes that sound?

It's all got to do with moving. For our muscles to work, they need two things – glucose and oxygen. This gives them their energy. We've seen how we get glucose into our blood through the digestive system but we also need to get oxygen into our blood.

Figure 1

Phew

Oxygen is a gas that is in all the air around us. There's plenty of oxygen in normal air so when we breathe we suck air into our body so that we can take some of the oxygen out of it. The air is sucked into our lungs – large soft sacks in your chest that are full of little pouches lined with tiny blood vessels. When the air gets into our lungs, oxygen is able to seep through the walls of these pouches and get into the blood.

At the same time our body needs to get rid of a waste gas called **carbon dioxide** so that is sent out the other way – out of the bloodstream into the pouches. When we breathe out, this waste gas is sent back out into the air around us.

Literacy

The **diaphragm** is a large sheet of muscle that seals your chest from your belly.

Carbon dioxide is a gas produced when oxygen is burned.

104

1 Air is sucked into the lungs when the ribs lift up and the diaphragm drops.

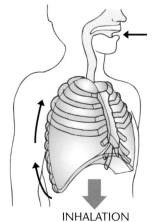

Air inhaled

2 Oxygen crosses into the bloodstream and carbon dioxide passes out.

INHALATION

Air exhaled

3 The ribs drop down and the diaphragm pulls tight and the air is squeezed out of the lungs back into the air.

EXHALATION

Figure 2

Activity

Put your hands on each side of your ribcage and feel what happens when you breathe in and out. Make a circle facing the same direction. Put your hands on the sides of the ribcage of the person in front of you. Count how many breaths they take while your teacher counts to ten, when you are standing at rest. Now all jog around in a circle for a minute and again count breaths for a count of ten. What did you notice about the two numbers?

When you move you are doing more work, your muscles need more oxygen and so you have to breathe more often to get the oxygen into your blood.

Swish

Blood has to carry the oxygen and food to the parts of your

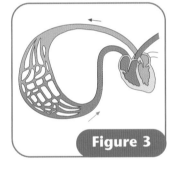

Figure 3

body that need it. The blood is made to move around your body in a series of tubes called **blood vessels**.

It starts in a big vessel leaves your lungs and goes straight to a two-sided pump called your heart. The blood is given a big push by the **heart** and is sent off around your body through arteries.

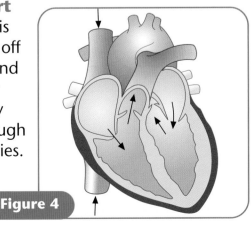

Figure 4

Blood travels along smaller arteries and these divide into smaller tubes called **capillaries** that go into every part of your body. Capillaries pass oxygen and glucose cross into the muscles and the water and carbon dioxide are carried away. The blood passes into larger tubes called veins. These carry it back to the other side of the heart, which in turn sends it back to the lungs again and round it goes again.

The heart keeps sending blood around the body to do its work – delivering food and oxygen and removing waste.

When you blush, capillaries bring blood close to the surface of the skin.

Figure 5

105

Figure 1

Look at this plant, can you name the parts that you can see?

I can see roots, stems, leaves and flowers but what do they all do?

In groups, see if you can write down what you think each part of the plant does.

 Plants and animals have similar needs –

1 water

2 an energy source

3 air

4 to get rid of wastes

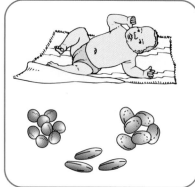

5 to make more like themselves

6 to be safe

Figure 2

A plant is a complicated factory.
Let's look at it as a flow chart.

Flowers made seeds.

Seeds leave the plant and make new plants where they land.

Leaves – these are the food factories. They make food from sunlight using a green chemical called **chlorophyll**. They have veins that carry water and food.

Stems carry water and food up and down the plant.

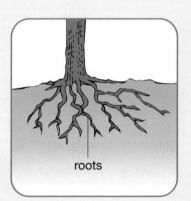

roots

Roots – this is where water and minerals are taken into the plant. They anchor the plant in place.

Did your group get the right answers?

Activity

How could you find out how quickly roots take up water? How could you find out where plants lose water from?

Why do animals need to move around yet plants usually stay in one place?

How many foods do you know that are plants or are made from plants? Write a list.

More than 90 thousand different kinds of living things live in Scotland. Most of them are very small and cannot be seen without a microscope. Others are difficult to find because they are very rare.

Case study 1. A rare Scottish plant – Scottish scurvygrass

Scurvygrass has been used for its healing properties for thousands of years. Scottish Scurvygrass with its white, cross-shaped flowers, lives in the north-west of Scotland. It is becoming rare – and this might be due to pollution or climate change. If it is lost altogether the other living things that depend on it for food will be affected.

Figure 1

Figure 2

Case study 2. A rare Scottish fish – the basking shark

The basking shark is the second largest fish in the world. It can be as long as 11 metres. It filters plankton from the water through its huge mouth.

Basking sharks are found around the west coast of Scotland in the Summer. The basking shark has been hunted for meat and the oil from its liver so that it is now very rare. It is a protected species. This means that laws have been passed to prevent people from killing, or even disturbing them. If this shark is lost altogether the other living things that depend on it for food will be affected.

Literacy

Plankton is tiny plant and animal life that is found in the sea.

Case study 3. A rare Scottish insect – the northern colletes

Figure 3

This rare bee – the northern colletes (Coll-eets) – is found on sandy **machair** grasslands on the North-west and island coast.

The northern colletes has become very rare due to the change of land use by farmers as well, possibly, to the effects of global warming. If this bee is lost altogether the other living things that depend on it for food will be affected.

Literacy

Machair is the Gaelic word for coastal grassland. The soil has lots of shell sand which is blown on to the land by strong winds from the beach.

Figure 4

Case study 4. A rare Scottish mammal – the bottlenose dolphin

Bottlenose dolphins live in warm water all around the world. They are related to whales and porpoises. Their beak makes them seem to be smiling. You do not need to travel far to see them since around 130 live in the Moray Firth. Thousands of tourists visit them every year. Although dolphins can live between 25 and 50 years they are becoming rarer because they get caught in fishing nets. If bottlenose dolphins are lost altogether the other living things that depend on it for food will be affected.

Case study 5. A rare Scottish bird – the corncrake

The corncrake is now rare throughout the world. They spend the winter in Africa and return to Scotland and other parts of Europe each spring for breeding. They hide in long grass but it is their rasping call that gives them away. Young birds are killed if the grass is cut too early. 'Corncrake-friendly' farming delays grass cutting on the Island of Coll to help these rare birds. The number of corncrakes has recently increased to around 600 in Scotland. If the corncrake is lost altogether the other living things that depend on it for food will be affected.

Figure 5

Key ideas

★ Many rare living things survive in Scotland and other parts of the world
★ They need our help to survive

Animals that are extinct

Did you know that wolves lived in Scotland until 300 years ago? Wolves are now **extinct** in Scotland.

Many Scottish towns have stories about wolves. Mary Queen of Scots once held a hunting match. Five wolves were killed as well as many deer. The burgh crest for the town of Stirling includes a wolf, celebrating the wolves that lived in nearby Wolf's Crag.

Wild boar, beavers and elk are other mammals that are now extinct in Scotland. They have been lost in recent times.

Literacy

Extinct means no longer existing.

Can you imagine a year ago? How about a thousand years ago? How about one hundred thousand or a million years ago – or 200 hundred million or even four hundred million years ago? Living things have been on Earth for about 550 million years!

**Earth timeline
One and fifty thousand years ago**

Cavemen like this lived on Earth and they hunted woolly mammoths and giant elk.

**Earth timeline
50 million years ago**

This dog sized forest creature fed on fruit and soft vegetation 50 million years ago. In time it has become the horse! As the climate changed over millions of years it became an animal adapted to those conditions, a larger, fast running animal of the plains.

Now

150,000 years ago   50 million years ago

Earth timeline
300 million years ago

During the Carboniferous period, East Kilbride in Scotland was on the equator. Scotland was joined to North America! During that period southern areas were often flooded by the sea. Sea creatures fossilized in the mud – sharks and other fish – are sometimes found.

Swamps covered the land with clubmoss forests. Giant centipedes, dragonflies and spiders were found there. The remains of the trees fall into the swamps, were buried and eventually fossilised into coal. These tree stumps were found in Victoria Park in Glasgow.

Lots of volcanoes were active in Scotland at that time – Arthur's Seat in Edinburgh was a volcano. The Campsie fells near Glasgow were also formed by volcanic lava.

Earth timeline
200 million years ago

During Jurassic times Scotland was very different from today. It was surrounded by a shallow, warm sea which was filled with strange sea life.

We know these lived here at that time because we found lots of their fossils. Dinosaurs lived on the land but only a few bones have been found in Scotland.

56 Protecting living things

Many living things are threatened with extinction. There are five main reasons for this.

Reason 1. The places where they live are being destroyed and removed

Birds that nest in trees, hedges, fields and marshes have their food and homes removed.

Figure 1

Forest has been planted in areas of Scotland and destroyed breeding areas for rare birds.

Reason 2. Climate change and global warming

 Flowering, insect hatching and bird migration happen at the same time each year. Scientists believe that global warming is affecting each of these and this is charging the balance of life.

Figure 2

As summers become warmer some butterfly species are moving north. Although the adults can breed in these areas the caterpillars might not find the right food.

Reason 3. Pollution

Chemicals can harm many living things and their food chains. The substances that are used to kill pests can poison their predators. Acid rain is caused by air pollution and damages forests.

Oil sometimes leaks from ships that carry it around the world. Oil on birds' feathers poisons them.

Figure 3

Reason 4. Persecution

Figure 4

 Millions of birds are shot each year during hunting seasons.

Figure 5

These beautiful red kites are persecuted in some areas of Scotland because some people believe they kill game birds.

Reason 5. Illegal trade

 Millions of wild animals are traded each year. They can be sold as pets, for their skins, to be used as medicine or food and even as souvenirs.

Figure 6

This elephant was killed for its ivory tusks.

Key ideas

★ Rare living things are under threat

★ They need our help to survive

113

This is Rory's bedroom. He doesn't take care of it. He throws rubbish on the floor instead of in the bin. He breaks things when he gets bored. He spills drinks on the carpet and writes on the walls. He plays wild games with his friends and this breaks the furniture.

He does not look after this environment and it will get worse until he decides to change his ways. It will cost a lot of money to replace the damaged furniture and carpet and re-decorate the walls.

Figure 1

Activity

How do you look after your room? In groups talk about things you do that look after your room and things you do are bad for your room. How do you feel about it? Do you get into trouble for things you do or are you very careful with your own space?

Your bedroom may be your own space or you might share it with one or two people. Perhaps your Mum or Dad come in and clear up your mess. How do you feel about that?

We are all responsible for a much bigger space around us – the environment outside your home – the place you live in, your school, your town, village or city and the countryside around it.

Activity

How do you treat the environment around you? Do you take care of it? Do you help to damage it by things you do? Do other people damage it and mess it up? Who do you think clears up after you and other people? Talk in groups about your feelings. Write down some of the good and bad things you could say about the environment you live in.

Could you change your behaviour to make sure you do less damage to the environment? Use some of the pictures below to get some ideas.

We also need to protect the animals in our environment.

Can you think of some simple things you could do to help animals in your environment?

Activity

In your group design and make a poster pledging some things you will try to do to protect the environment you live in.

WE WILL TRY TO PROTECT OUR ENVIRONMENT BY:

1. ... ...

In the summer we wear light clothes to keep cool. In the winter we wear warm clothes to keep warm. We change how we dress to suit the weather.

Figure 1

We live in places that are suitable for our lives. We do not live on mountaintops because they are too cold, windy and don't have a good water supply. We don't live in a marsh because it is too wet. We live in houses built in places that make it easier for us to survive. Think about the area you live in. What makes it a good area for you to survive in?

Animals and plants also live in areas that suit them.

Plants such as grass and heather can live on mountaintops because they are low to the ground and are able to limit the amount of water they lose. They can live well despite the wind and cold conditions.

Figure 3

Figure 4

These plants are happy living with their roots in water and the frog needs to be in damp places to survive so they can all live happily in marshy areas.

Figure 2

Figure 5

Look at the animals in this picture. How many can you name? Each of them lives here because it is a good place to live and has the things they need to survive.

The squirrel lives up a tree so cats and other predators can't reach it. It stores nuts in the Autumn so that it has  food in the winter. It grows a thicker coat in the winter to keep it warm.

 The blackbird lives in thick bushes and uses its sharp beak to poke about for grubs and insects to eat. It loves fruit that has fallen from a tree and is starting to rot and so often lives in gardens and parks where there are fruit trees. Its eyes allow it to see all around so that if danger threatens it can quickly fly away and be safe. The bushes provide a safe place for it to make its nest and lay eggs.

The mouse is very small and quick. It is brown in colour and so is hidden when in amongst plants and leaves – we call this camouflage. It can eat all sorts of things – berries, stalks and crumbs – and so finds lots of food in the park. It hides away in a hole  until it needs to feed, often only coming out at night when there is no one about.

The tree lives here because it has room to grow. There is good soil for it to spread its roots and by growing above  the other plants it can get all the sunlight it needs. Its branches are bendy so that it does not break in the wind. In winter it drops its leaves so that it can survive the cold weather.

Grass can grow well here because it is an open area so it gets lots of sunlight. It can survive being cut regularly through the summer and that actually makes it grow faster. It has good soil so that its roots grow well and keep it anchored in the ground. It gets water from the soil and if it is very dry in the summer it stops growing and dies back but the roots stay alive so that when it gets water it can start to grow again. The leaves are quite tough so it can stand being walked on.

What sort of animals live in or visit your playground?

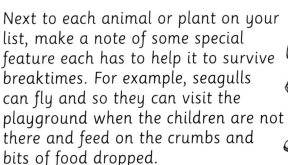

Activity

 In your group, write a list of animals (including birds, minibeasts, mammals etc.) and plants that might live in or visit your playground.

The playground is quite a dangerous place for some living things – lots of children appear several times a day, running about, kicking balls, skipping and playing. Look at your list of living things. How do they survive playtimes?

What special way of living do they have that allows them to live there or visit?

Next to each animal or plant on your list, make a note of some special feature each has to help it to survive breaktimes. For example, seagulls can fly and so they can visit the playground when the children are not there and feed on the crumbs and bits of food dropped.

59

Unsuitable pets

 Dogs and cats are popular pets. So are hamsters and goldfish.

Some people like to keep unusual wild animals as pets. They do not realise that many animals are not suitable pets.

Figure 1

It is illegal to buy and sell endangered species.

Wild animals need special food and places to live.

They often die during capture or when they are transported.

Wild animals do not survive while in captivity.

Figure 2

Health and animal science

 Science helps us to understand living things. Medical science helps us understand how diseases can be controlled with medicines. Animals are sometimes used in experiments to find out more about those medicines. Some people think this is unnecessary. What do you think?

Alternatives to pets

Instead of keeping animals as pets, why not volunteer or join organisations that care for animals or support wildlife clubs.

Scotland's national parks

Most of us accept that the environment must be protected. Science will help us to preserve nature and make it available to future generations. Scotland now has two National Parks – around Loch Lomond and the Cairngorms.
These aim to:

- Conserve and understand nature and culture

- Provide enjoyment

- Promote local development

Figure 3

We make choices that are in the interest of wildlife. These must also take note of the how those decisions affect other people's jobs and other aspects of society. Everyone should help to make these important decisions.

Figure 4

60

How does your garden grow?

The gang are looking at their lawn. It's looking a bit untidy.

Figure 1

Is there a piece of grass in your school grounds that you know well? Do you think what any of the gang says is true for your piece of grass?

How could you find out? Get together in your groups and talk about your ideas.

The gang are going to look at their lawn closely to find out who is right. They have put a tape measure across the lawn from one side to the other.

They are going to use a 'window' made from cardboard to see how many different types of plants there are in the lawn at different points along the tape.

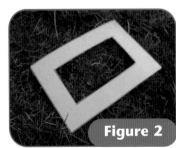

Figure 2

Figure 3

They are writing down how many different types they find at each spot. They move along the tape 1 metre at a time.

Their results look look this –

Distance along tape/metres	1	2	3	4	5
Number of types of plant – set 1	10	8	5	6	9

Was this a fair test? What should they do to see if there is a pattern?

Mairi moved the tape measure further along the lawn.

They repeated what they did three times in three different places across the lawn. This table shows these results:

Distance along tape/metres	1	2	3	4	5
Number of types of plant – set 2	12	5	5	6	6
Number of types of plant – set 3	3	4	6	5	8

Look at the picture of the where the tape was for the third set of results.

Figure 4

In your groups, thinks about these results and draw some block graphs to show the distance from the drive against the number of different plants found.

Is there a pattern about the number of plant types and the distance from the drive? Can you think of why this could be? Can you say anything else about the number of plant types in the lawn? Do you notice anything else? Can you try this yoruself?

Figure 4

Index